RUMINATION REMEDIES

A WORKBOOK

to free your mind from

Worry, Regret, and Racing Thoughts

SHERI McGREGOR, M.A.

Copyright © 2025 Sheri McGregor

All rights reserved. No part of this publication may be reproduced, distributed, or transmitted in any form or by any means, including photocopying, recording, or other electronic or mechanical methods, without the prior written permission of the publisher, except in the case of brief quotations embodied in critical reviews and certain other noncommercial uses permitted by copyright law. For permission requests, write to the publisher, addressed "Attention: Permissions Coordinator," at the address below.

ISBN: 978-0-9973522-7-6 (print)
ISBN: 978-0-9973522-8-3 (ebook)

SEL016000   SELF-HELP / Personal Growth / Happiness
SEL024000   SELF-HELP / Self-Management / Stress Management
SEL031000   SELF-HELP / Personal Growth / General

Sowing Creek Press
Shingle Springs, CA 95692
info@sowingcreekpress.com
www.SowingCreekPress.com

DISCLAIMER:
This book is not a substitute for medical, spiritual, legal, or psychological advice. Content is based on the author's personal experience, as well as studies and research, but is the author's opinion. Readers should contact a licensed physician, psychiatrist, psychologist, or other licensed practitioner for diagnosis and care, or an attorney for legal advice. Although care was taken to ensure the research and information in this book was correct at the time it went to press, the author and publisher do not assume and hereby disclaim any liability to any party for loss, damage, or disruption due to any errors or omissions—whether the result of negligence, accident, or any other cause.

Cover and page design/layout by Lorie DeWorken, MindtheMargins.com

Praise for *Rumination Remedies*

"If rumination has ever hijacked your peace of mind, this book is your roadmap back to calm. In *Rumination Remedies*, Sheri McGregor offers 41 powerful, practical tools to help you recognize, interrupt, and release repetitive thought loops. Each remedy is clearly explained—with the "why it works," detailed how-to steps, and plenty of real-life examples—so you're not just reading, you're actually practicing and experiencing change. Whether you're lying awake with worry, replaying conversations, or bracing for what-ifs, this workbook gives you the tools to take back control. Thoughtfully written, immediately useful, and deeply compassionate—this is a must-have for anyone ready to stop spinning and start living with more ease and clarity."

—LORI CLEMMONS
Author of *Rewire Your Wellness: A Guide For Reclaiming Your Life from Chronic Illness, Anxiety, and Pain*

"If you want to quiet your mind and quell your circular, endless-loop thinking habits to achieve greater peace and happiness, then this inspirational workbook RUMINATION REMEDIES is the must-have manual for you. Multi-Award Winning author Sheri McGregor, of the *Done With The Crying* series of books for parents of estranged adult children, among numerous other acclaimed books and literary publications, brilliantly and masterfully offers creative, easy-to-implement techniques and measurable action steps for identifying our triggers and reframing our often self-destructive, repetitive inner thoughts, regrets and worries to become more positive, productive and peaceful. With thoughtful, gentle encouragement and realistic remedies, written in a practical style, yet with a flexible format leaving room for variation and personal choice, which includes tangible ideas, relatable examples and space to document our responses and reflections, we can release and reel-in our destructive pattern of rumination once and for all. Prepare to be transformed: mind, body and soul."

—DR. MARNI HILL FODERARO
Multi-award winning author of *God Came To My Garage Sale*, *Parental Alienation* and the book series *TRUE DECEIT FALSE LOVE*

"I love this book. In *Rumination Remedies*, Sheri McGregor offers 41 evidence-based strategies to interrupt overthinking and restore calm, each grounded in neuroscience and infused with deep compassion. She draws from a wide range of proven practices: vagal nerve stimulation, intentional change theory, awe and gratitude exercises, embodiment and mindful movement, cold exposure, self-talk reframing, nature-based practices, and more. The breadth of these approaches means everyone will find several that resonate and can make a meaningful difference in their lives. This is more than a workbook; it is a guide to reclaiming presence, cultivating resilience, and building new neural pathways for peace and clarity."

—Irena O'Brien, PhD
Founder, The Neuroscience School
Host of the podcast "Neuroscience of Coaching"

Author's Note to Readers

As a kid growing up with a dad who worried about everything, I learned at an early age just how miserable overthinking can be. Much of Dad's energy went to imagining fretful scenarios that never actually transpired. Or, he turned over incidents that had already happened. In some ways, his suffering spread to the rest of the family as he tried to keep us safe. I saw my dad's turmoil and vowed not to be like that. Genetics, learned behavior, and some devastating life blows have tested that vow—*and made it stronger.*

It's helpful to ponder how things turned out in order to process emotions and learn for the future. That's different than a tyranny of overthinking that holds you hostage, steals your sleep, peace, and joy. My coaching clients report that rumination is a major obstacle that diminishes confidence and prevents them from taking charge of their lives. That I've witnessed this problem in so many others, experienced and overcame its effects myself motivated me to write this book—*for you.*

Each of us has an inner landscape we can enrich with creativity, beauty, and joy. In the pages ahead, you'll be encouraged to mentally travel back in time to memories worth savoring, to look forward in blissful anticipation, and to rest your mind, grounded in the present. The remedies are practical, based in research, and allow for your personalization.

If you find this workbook useful, please spread the word. Tell friends you believe will benefit. Form book groups where members work through the remedies on their own—and then meet to share insights and celebrate success. You *can* overcome rumination. I hope you'll share your experience in online reviews so we can all savor the cultivated landscape of your unique and beautiful mind.

RUMINATION REMEDIES

TABLE OF CONTENTS

Author's Note to Readers 5
Introduction 11
Remedy 1: Say What? 15
Remedy 2: Your Turnaround 23
Remedy 3: *Learning Curve,* Your Wi-Fi 29
Remedy 4: Watch Your Tone 35
Remedy 5: Who's That You're Talking To? 41
Remedy 6: Wee-Hour Check-in 45
Remedy 7: Shift into Neutral 49
Remedy 8: The Shake Break 53
Remedy 9: Pattern Interrupt 55
Remedy 10: Cherished Evidence 61
Remedy 11: Message to Self—Chill Out 65
Remedy 12: *Learning Curve,* A Five-Star Review 67
Remedy 13: Making Tomorrow Real 73
Remedy 14: N-E-W 79
Remedy 15: You're Here Now, and Safe 83
Remedy 16: Awestruck 91
Remedy 17: Fresh Eyes 97
Remedy 18: What Would Batman, Jesus, or the Dalai Lama Do? . . . 101
Remedy 19: *Thrival,* It's in Your Genes 105
Remedy 20: A Routine to Remember 109

Remedy 21: The Mother's Touch 115
Remedy 22: *Learning Curve*, Building Bridges 119
Remedy 23: Pour It Out 123
Remedy 24: Say It to the Dolls 133
Remedy 25: Normalize 137
Remedy 26: *Solvitur Ambulando* 141
Remedy 27: Touchstones and Talismans 147
Remedy 28: Tidy Up 151
Remedy 29: In Flow 157
Remedy 30: A Sigh of Relief 161
Remedy 31: *Learning Curve*, Body in Mind 165
Remedy 32: Tune in and Tune Out 169
Remedy 33: P-R-O-C-E-E-D 177
Remedy 34: Bend Your Ear? 183
Remedy 35: Worst-Case Scenario 187
Remedy 36: Your B-F-F 191
Remedy 37: Real Eyes for Peace 197
Remedy 38: Bust a Move 201
Remedy 39: Viva Las *Vagus!* 205
Remedy 40: *Learning Curve*, The Wrap-Up 207
Remedy 41: Congratulate Yourself! 213
About the Author 217
Endnotes 219

Introduction

Some of my earliest memories include my dad teasing me about my endless chatter. He'd ask, *"Who wound you up?"* Then, he'd press an imaginary OFF button at the back of my neck. As an adult, I've lain awake with an overactive mind and asked myself the same question. At times, I've longed for an OFF button to quiet my inner talk.

Of all the side effects that go with stress and the breakdown of cherished relationships, the wound-up circular thinking that steals your peace is among the worst. Painful incidents replay and mix with future uncertainty on an endless loop that leaves you exhausted and feeling out of control.

What did he mean by that? Why did I say that? I wish I'd said … What can I do now? Will it always be this way? What will people think? How am I going to fit that commitment in? I should have said yes. I should have said no. Why can't I ever say no? I wish he would… I can't believe that she… I forgot to do that… Who do I think I am to try this? Why did I ever agree? Now, I'll fail and …

Self-doubt leads to self-blame and hopelessness. Sleep is elusive. Inner peace seems impossible. *Where's the OFF button?*

Rumination is torture. I've had my share. You probably have, too. That's why I've created this easy-to-use workbook. Inside, you'll find a series of techniques to help you gain control and be kinder to yourself.

Rumination Defined

The word "ruminate" derives from a centuries-old Latin variant that means to "chew the cud." This makes sense because "rumen" is the English word for the first of four stomachs found in animals that chew a cud. Multiple stomachs help cows and other ruminant animals to break down their diet of coarse grass. There's a purpose to the process, which is the opposite of chewing the same old emotionally draining cud (or *crud!*). That kind of chewing is not meant for the human mind. It gets you nowhere.

Self-recrimination, racing worries, or raging regret... No matter what the content, negative thinking can become a habit, and even *bad* habits are something we can count on when our world feels topsy-turvy. If you're in the habit of thinking negatively—when you're trying to get to sleep, when you're stressed, or whenever some trigger sets you off—it's time to recognize rumination for what it is, an emotional rut, and bid the old habit good-bye.

Using This Workbook

In the pages ahead, you'll find a cabinet full of tried-and-true remedies. Each exercise is presented with lead-in scenarios that convey understanding and engage interest. I've included research, real-life stories, and reflection points. Yet the workbook isn't bogged down with explanations. *Rumination Remedies* is experiential, meaning you learn in the doing, so it becomes more of a *play*book than a *work*book. You'll use your identified thinking patterns and unique dilemmas to make these transformative techniques your own. You *can* take charge of your mind and regain a sense of peace.

The first two remedies set the stage for your success. Take your time, observe your thinking, and patiently participate with the material. Build a strong foundation. Beyond those, each remedy is intended for your practice over several days to a week and includes space to record your thoughts and experiences as you use the techniques. Don't skimp on your reflections. Your mind is vying for your attention. This is a chance to give it some loving care. Get involved with your thinking and get to know yourself better. You count.

To solidify what's learned, I've sprinkled *Learning Curves* throughout the book. When you answer the questions, use the checklists, and reflect as directed in these sections, you'll gain additional insights and information that help you measure and maintain your progress. The most effective helping tools are those you rely upon and turn to often. To do that you must know them well—and know how you respond to them. The *Learning Curves* will help you note resistance, record helpful adjustments, and celebrate your success.

Among the remedies that focus directly on your mind are techniques that work with your body and breath. These aim to increase mind-body connection as well as tone your vagus nerve, which plays an important role in well-being. The vagus nerve runs from the brain through the heart, lungs, and digestive system. When vagal tone is low, the central nervous system is less resilient, and your ruminating mind reflects that. Higher vagal tone helps you shift more easily between the fight-or-flight response of stress to the calm state known as rest-and-digest. A well-toned vagus nerve enhances overall well-being and emotional control, which help you discard unhelpful thinking.

No single way of using this book is right for everyone. You can skip ahead or pick and choose exercises that most appeal to you. For the best results, I recommend following the remedies from start to finish. That way, you'll ease into implementing and refining the techniques to suit your needs over the course of each week. You'll develop a routine of reading, practicing, and recording unique results that will serve your continued progress.

Bring an Open Mind

With a heaping dose of self-compassion, you'll increase your self-control and start to gain confidence. Enlist a curious attitude as you play your way through the book. Your interaction with the remedies at this time in your life makes them unique to your present needs. I've added lots of alternative ideas in *Additional Tips and Techniques* sections and left plenty of room for you to reshape and individualize the material to fit your needs. As you progress through the practices, be *all in* for yourself and your well-being. You'll invite your inner wisdom to come out and play.

Cultivate a spirit of openness. Give tips you may not be immediately drawn to a chance. You'll learn more about yourself and expand your skills as you go. The exercises are intended to build upon each other. Deeply rooting in the information, and paying close attention to your experiences with the remedies, will aid neuroplasticity, which is your brain's natural solution to changing unhelpful habits.

You may find that a particular exercise and its reflection points bring up old incidents and memories. Ruminating may skate the surface and, as such, prevent the helpful processing of emotions. As your negative thinking habits change, you may find that you're ready to do richer work toward deeper healing. This workbook isn't a substitute for personalized care and support.

As you begin this workbook, remember that you're not alone. Close your eyes for a moment and imagine all the very real people all around the world who are working to reclaim their happiness and joy. Together, you create an atmosphere of synergy and healing.

Free your mind, feel more confident, and function more effectively. You'll need a few months to complete *Rumination Remedies*. The time will be well spent. Don't be surprised if you start to feel better immediately.

Remedy 1

Say What?

Initial Notes

Before beginning this exercise, read the instructions all the way through. They're short, thorough, and will help you succeed. You'll be engaging in this first step for at least several days, so it's important to be clear on expectations—and then to follow through. Give yourself the gift of your own focus, discipline, and care. You're worth your own time and energy.

This exercise is written with broad strokes. Even if you're not currently struggling with rumination, you can gain insight from familiar thought loops that will help with future bouts. If you're actively struggling, use your current episodes. If not, be grateful! And ... choose a time when you can safely think back to more troubling times and ask yourself the same sorts of questions listed for active rumination (below).

Why This Remedy Works

Without awareness, you're just groping around in the dark. The first step toward freeing your mind is to lay a concrete foundation for inner peace. That means getting up close and personal with your thoughts. Noticing and recording specifics will help you to:

- identify details about what prompts rumination
- recognize the particulars of content
- observe any negative consequences

How to Use This Remedy

You'll need to get in touch with three important elements of your thinking: content, prompts, and effects. They'll dovetail as you complete the exercise.

The "Content"

Over the next several days, become aware of your thoughts. Whether active, prolonged rumination, or simply your automatic self-talk, notice what you tell yourself. This means friendly self-talk as well as anything negative. Pats on your own back are as valuable for gaining insight as a harsher inner critic. Take note of everything from, "Wow, I got so much done today," to "I'm such an idiot." Also, note what situations prompt your inner talk. In this way, you get used to *actively* hearing your own voice. The next exercise in this workbook will build on this idea, but for now, noticing and recording are most important. We all talk to ourselves, but we don't necessarily listen or become truly aware.

In addition to your routine inner chatter, notice any times your mind won't shut down. You know, the gnawing *What-if . . .? Why-did-I ...? and How-could-s/he ...?* -type thinking that relentlessly repeats and interferes with productivity, socializing, mood, and sleep. Notice and record what you're thinking. Are you worried about the future? Berating yourself for a lack of control? Wishing you'd have done this or that differently or better? What's the narrative? What, exactly, are you telling (or asking) yourself? And don't forget tone and cadence. Is the voice in your head shrill, breathy, cheerful, distressed, whiney, excited, crying, angry . . .? Are your thoughts racing, sluggish, halting . . . ?

The "Prompts"

Equally important as the content is to consider the prompts, sometimes also called "triggers." As you record your thinking, be sure to identify and note what situations, people, conversations, news, or activities started up your unhelpful inner dialogue or ruminative episodes.

Here, we're aiming more for the present moment than identifying an overarching situation. You might immediately think of more global reasons such as, "My adult child is estranged." Or, "I should never have married him/her." Or, "I gave up my career for ..." The idea is to drill down further. Did interacting with a friend/relative who has the "perfect" family set you off? Was it looking at your ex's social media? Were you praised for an accomplishment? Or did a "friend's" questions send your mind spinning into uncontrollable territory? Perhaps a nosey neighbor prompted uneasy feelings and you self-protected by not divulging the whole truth. Your rumination has its own history. Uncovering the prompts forms a basis for your future peace of mind.

The "Effects"

How does your self-talk make you feel? Happy, sad, out of control . . . ? In what way does ruminating affect your behavior? Perhaps you're less productive or avoid social situations. Take note of negative effects. Do you:

- doubt yourself?
- lose sleep?
- overwork?
- indulge in unhealthy eating (or other habits)?

Additional Tips and Techniques

To Catch Yourself Thinking:

Sometimes people don't catch themselves until they're knee-deep in rumination. If you find this frequently happens to you, set up some help to become more aware. A trusted companion might be willing to stop you now and again and ask, "Penny for your thoughts?" Sharing isn't required. Use the prompt to tune into your thoughts. Other reminder prompts include setting your phone's alarm to go off periodically. Or choose a random trigger such as every time your cat meows, a new text arrives, or you hear your neighbor's sink turn on in the apartment next door. Anything that happens frequently but not constantly could work. Get creative. You know your life and what would make sense.

To Record Your Thoughts:

Send yourself texts as the thoughts appear. Or open a computer file if that's more convenient. You could also choose to speak your details into a recording app. This work is important, so use what is convenient and makes the most sense for you. It's easiest if all your notes are in one place. So, if you're using alternatives, transcribe these into workbook pages, a journal, or somewhere else that aids organization.

On the lines below, you'll begin to record your self-talk and rumination. To ease into the work, think about your thought patterns, worries, and self-talk in a general manner as you answer the questions.

- How and when do you talk to yourself? Is your inner voice kind? Or do you tend to berate yourself?

_____

_____

_____

_____

_____

_____

- What prompts your self-talk and rumination?

_____

_____

_____

_____

_____

_____

- What are the effects on you?

___

Now that you've reflected in a general manner, let's get more detailed. Over the next several days, make a practice of observing your inner dialogue. Then capture your thoughts in real time. Use the lines to record your self-talk and rumination. Be specific in the content. Also, be sure to identify and note what prompted the self-talk, thoughts, or ruminative episodes. Note the tone, cadence, and how the thinking made you feel. What were any effects on your mood and/or behavior?

___

> "Thoughts, like birds, came fluttering to her heart."
> — *Louisa May Alcott* (1832–1888)

Remedy 2

Your Turnaround

Initial Notes
Now that you have a basic handle on content, prompts, and the impact of your self-talk and rumination on your well-being, you're better equipped to make positive changes. There's no need to rush. We're still working on the foundation to reshape and calm your inner life. We'll focus on three steps: Celebrating, narrowing in, and compassionately reframing your cogitation.

Why This Remedy Works
The work done to celebrate wins and compassionately reframe negativity has several benefits. You will:

- understand yourself better
- increase confidence
- decrease anxiety
- strengthen productive thinking habits
- feel more motivated and happier [1, 2, 3]

How to Use This Remedy

PART ONE: *Celebrate*

Many of us go from one accomplishment to the next, never pausing to bask in the warmth of success. We shift immediately to whatever's next. Or we discount our progress with negative self-talk like, "It's about time," or "I should have done that sooner."

Acknowledging and celebrating your wins help you understand what worked so you can repeat the actions that led to success. While this may not directly connect to rumination, consider that remedies intended for a primary purpose often have positive effects in other areas. Quitting smoking is better for your health (primary goal) *and* your breath smells sweeter (secondary gain). A medication prescribed for one problem sometimes inadvertently fixes another. Let celebrating and savoring your feel-good moments and learning from your wins be secondary gains here. Practice will make this second nature.

Review your notes from Remedy One (*Say What?*) and look for any times you celebrated and cheered yourself on. On the lines below, note what prompted the feel-good self-talk you recorded. Take a moment to savor the memory. As you reflect, notice your physical sensations. Allow yourself to smile, breathe in the satisfaction, and tell yourself again, "I'm doing great," or "That was a fantastic job," or "I did good!" Write your congratulatory phrases next to each item.

Additional Tips and Techniques

> To foster future success, at some point, jot down some notes about steps taken, support sought, schedule followed, or whatever else contributed to your success. Did you remain calm during a tough conversation? Celebrate and savor that success. Then record what contributed to your win. Did you take care of physical needs to support your stable emotional baseline? Did you schedule the talk at a time and place that felt right? Make notes for each item.

Note: If you didn't record any feel-good moments in Remedy One, don't beat yourself up. You're becoming aware. That's important, and Part Three of this exercise will get you primed to more consciously engage in encouraging, beneficial self-talk. Still, pause now and reflect. List some things you're proud of, no matter how long ago or small.

"Self-knowledge includes the courage to own your virtues
as well as your faults."
— *Charlotte Perkins Gilman* (1860–1935)

PART TWO: *Narrow In*

Review your notes from Remedy One and reflect on the times your inner chatter was critical, negative, or harsh. What prompted those thoughts? Use the lines below to reflect upon these questions: What harsh, critical, or negative words and phrases did you use? What was your tone? Were you rushed, angry, or sad? Did you call yourself names? Was your rumination frantic, fearful, or whiney? Was your inner dialogue desperate, hopeless, or pleading?

PART THREE: *Compassionately Reframe*

Here's where we begin shifting negative thoughts: *Your Turnaround*. To get you started, I've listed a few generic examples of unhelpful self-talk followed by compassionate reframing of the statements. After studying the examples, turn to the negativity you recorded in Remedy One and just now reflected upon. On the lines below, rewrite your negative words and add your own turnarounds.

You'll be returning to your affirming statements later, so make them easy to differentiate. Use a highlighter or a different colored ink pen. You could also draw a line down center to create two columns, writing negative statements on the left and affirmations on the right. Even then, added color will make the self-talk you're aiming for stand out on the page. Take your time with this exercise. As new negativity comes to mind over the course of several days to a week, add those thoughts and your turnarounds.

Examples:

If my own child doesn't like me, I must be pretty bad.	*Other people like me. My wife/husband, my sister, my friend... all appreciate me. One person's opinion doesn't determine my likeability or define who I am.*
I'm such a failure.	*I succeed at many things. I continue to work at bettering myself.*
I said "no" this time. What if s/he never invites me again?	*I was wise to prioritize my own needs and take care of myself. I can reach out when it's right for me.*
What if I never get another chance?	*I can make my own opportunities in life.*
I'm scared this will never change.	*I am learning to adapt as life unfolds. I can create new situations that suit me.*
I'm such a dope.	*I'm learning every day.*

_____

_____

_____

Remedy 3

Learning Curve, Your Wi-Fi

Initial Notes
In the first two remedies, you analyzed the content of your ruminative thinking and identified what prompts the episodes. You also began to reframe your thinking in a more positive light. Don't forget to celebrate any success so far. You'll have the chance to do that in future *Learning Curve* sessions, too. Now it's time to consider how your negative thinking has affected you and to define your "desired outcomes" (goals).

Why This Remedy Works
Knowing what motivates you, that is, knowing the meaningful reasons why you take specific actions toward goals, is like igniting a furnace deep inside you. Focusing on your *why* (Wi) sustains the fire (Fi) that fuels necessary work for positive change—even when the tasks are difficult, and the going is tough. We'll call this your personal "Wi-Fi." Writing out your desired outcomes (goals) will improve your confidence, build motivation, and increase your achievement rate.[1,2]

Let's Get Started
Almost everywhere you go these days, there's an invisible force working behind the scenes: Wi-Fi. The signal connects to our smart phones, keeps our apps dinging with reminders and, in some ways, makes our lives easier. Our behavior, including how we think, can be similar.

Long ago, you may have formed thinking patterns that continue to exert pressure without your full awareness, pinging old alarms that trigger and replay negative thought patterns. Remedies One and Two began making you more aware of what motivates your negative thinking. This time, you'll identify and concentrate on upgraded motivation for more helpful cognition. Think of this exercise like getting new, up-to-speed Wi-Fi that powers you forward.

Here, I'm referring to your "Wi-Fi" as an easy-to-recall term to help you remain focused and energized. Your Wi-Fi stokes the internal resources you'll need to continue experimenting with the workbook techniques and drop habitual thinking that no longer serves you.

The first step is to commit the term to memory.

Talk to yourself out loud. Say: *Your why is your fire. Your Wi-Fi.*

Now write it out. *Your why is your fire. Your Wi-Fi.*

The second step is to look over your notes about the content of your thoughts and what prompts them. Then think of desired outcomes. For instance, do you often make self-critical statements and judge yourself for things you said or did earlier (or didn't say or do)? This could happen in conversation or when you let opportunities pass you by. Later, you think of everything you should have said and berate yourself for being such a dolt. The desired outcomes (goals) would be to stop judging yourself so harshly and to give yourself more compassion. That kinder inner voice is more confidence-building and motivating than the beat-down of your unforgiving inner critic.

Now let's explore your *why* (Wi) which feeds your motivating fire (Fi). Perhaps you realize that, in criticizing yourself, you decrease your self-esteem. Your critical judgment may then result in you also tolerating others' disrespect. Or perhaps your self-critical thinking loop tamps your confidence so low that you won't take any risk. You're far less likely to speak up or try anything new if you're telling yourself that you always fail, aren't clever enough, or some other self-defeating prophecy (that becomes self-sabotaging action or inaction). By not trying, you protect yourself from external disappointment, but you also limit your possibility to enjoy life to the fullest. Your Wi (*why*) may be about increasing self-confidence for better presence, performance, and opportunity.

Your self-defeating behavior can also limit the people around you. So your motivating *why* may have to do with them. For example, if you're always telling yourself that you don't fit in or don't know what to say, supporting your loved one by going along to an important social event may become difficult. Your *why*, then, may relate to a desire to make progress against your self-defeating thinking and consider yourself a better partner, worker, or friend.

Getting down on yourself decreases your happiness and hope. Who can enjoy life when there's nothing to feel grateful for or look forward to? Your Wi-Fi, then, is a more positive and hopeful outlook, which can bolster relationships, bring joy, and make living more fun. Your Wi-Fi may be all the real experiences you open up to, which will expand your life.

As another example, consider negative thinking that keeps you up at night. Lack of sleep contributes to physical illness, irritability, low energy, and mood. Better sleep becomes your Wi-Fi. Ahead, you'll experiment with specific remedies and discover which tools best help you enjoy better sleep (or what fits your *why*).

Widening out now, do you have other people counting on you? Do you need lots of energy to do meaningful work of some kind? Is there a dream you've been holding close and now have time to pursue? These sorts of questions bring your Wi-Fi into view. Don't let negative thinking, worry, or rumination get in the way. That's what the rest of this workbook will help you overcome.

On the lines below, reflect upon what you value most at this point in your life. Is it your marriage? Your work? Your pets? Consider what gives you meaning. Write out your thoughts. Don't censor yourself. We are all unique. Honesty with yourself is vital for growth.

_____

_____

_____

_____

_____

_____

_____

_____

_____

_____

Now that you've completed some reflective writing, you'll succinctly pen a few desired outcomes and your Wi-Fis. You can have many, and this will make them easy to return to later and use to re-energize. Drawing from the examples, write out your goals and motivation in short form for easy Wi-Fi reboot.

Examples:

Goal: *Stop ruminating at night and sleep better.*

Wi-Fi: *Good sleep fuels physical wellness, which enhances a calmer, fuller presence with people and at work. The benefits are increased productivity, good feelings about yourself, better relationships, and physical and mental wellness.*

Goal: *More control over your thinking.*

Wi-Fi: *A fretting mind drowns out fun. More control of thoughts aids being fully present with loved ones. This increases enjoyment of time together and allows for more spontaneity and fun. That's healthy for all relationships.*

_____

_____

_____

_____

_____

_____

_____

_____

> "The secret of achievement is to keep alive in yourself
> the motive that first set you upon the work."
> —*Mary Lyon* (1797–1849)

Remedy 4

Watch Your Tone

Initial Notes

When communicating with others, we often modulate our tone and rate of speech to fit the person or the message we want to convey. We shift our pitch and volume, add gestures, pauses, and even move our body to demonstrate eagerness, sincerity, or care. This "paralanguage" consists of the parts of communicating that go beyond the content, and good communicators learn early on how to better persuade, defuse situations, or convey emotions.

To motivate a team member who made a mistake, we might brush the air with our hand as if sweeping away doubt, and say, "It was just one time. Don't let it get you down." We might then make a fist and assuredly cheer, "You've got this. I've seen how well you play." Or, "We're in this together."

Compare that to how we interact with an injured child. With a tilt of our head and perhaps even a pout, we'll talk sweetly, drawing out well-chosen words or sounds to indicate empathy and care. "Aw-*aw* ... Doggone it ... that *hurts*. Come here, sweetie. Let me have a look."

Likewise, a spooked horse requires gentle tones and slow movements to elicit trust. We lower our pitch and speak slowly, demonstrating we're not a threat and have all the time in the world. "Ea-sy now, Dusty."

So why is it that, when it comes to ourselves, so many of us stub a toe and hiss, "Stupid! I don't have time for this." We might even further berate ourselves: "Every time I'm in a hurry, I do some dumb move to make myself late. What the hell is wrong with me?" Not only are our words harsh, but so is our pitch. We directly demean our intelligence or imply that we're inept.

35

Gosh, what the heck is wrong with us?

We would do well to pay attention to how we treat ourselves and offer more self-respect and kindness, not only in our words, but in our paralanguage. If we're asking why we always stub a toe or do some other "dumb move" when we're in a hurry and already late, maybe there's something to learn. A parent might interpret a child's tarrying before school as a possible sign of a problem such as feeling insecure or being bullied, and then softly ask the child what's up. We can give ourselves the same courtesy in our questioning and perhaps have an aha moment that helps us grow.

Asking ourselves sincere questions in a spirit of self-directed kindness can be an effective way to learn something important. Thinking, *Hmm. Why is it that I'm so frequently running late?* may yield answers. Maybe you're packing too much into the evenings and need to adjust your nighttime schedule or change some other habit. Perhaps you're often running late because you're feeling wary of a new responsibility, you dread seeing someone, or you resent having agreed to go to an event.

Caring questions that reveal useful insights are more productive than any snakelike hiss. Harsh, accusatory self-talk, whether in a question or statement format, only amps up our central nervous system, adding to our stress. Whether our inner voice is reacting in the moment or we're lying in bed ruminating, learning to purposely choose *how* we talk to ourselves will help.

Shift your pitch to one of empathy. "Aw, honey, this is hard, isn't it?" You could hug yourself, clasp your hands together, or rest your hands on your heart as you tell yourself gently, "Let's see if you can let it go." Intentionally shift your body language, tone, and content to calm your nervous system rather than raise alarm bells. You'll think more clearly.

Why This Remedy Works

Becoming aware of the tone, cadence, and various other features in *how* we talk to ourselves, beyond just the content, helps us put ourselves at ease. When we speak in a kinder way to ourselves, we can access better reasoning and gain information that's obscured by knee-jerk reactions. We can reduce stress and take better care of ourselves.

Additional Tips and Techniques

Especially if your self-talk is sharp-edged and hurtful, thinking about where you learned the behavior can help. Maybe impatient people have treated you this way in the past—and standing up for yourself would have been unsafe for you. What works to maintain belonging and survival at one point in this life isn't necessarily useful forever. Do you still allow others to speak to you in such ways? Awareness is a first step toward positive change. Or, perhaps you witnessed your parents or other loved ones treating *themselves* this way—and picked up the habit. Regardless of the reasons, do yourself a favor and ditch these negative habits.

Note: If your inner voice is soft, patient, and kind, does it remind you of anyone? If so, savor the memory of someone who cared. Jot down a few thoughts. Then, be cognizant of carrying that person's loving kindness more purposefully forward to yourself and others.

_____

_____

_____

_____

_____

How to Use This Remedy

The task is to notice the *how*, the paralanguage of your ruminative episodes or reactive self-talk. And then work to shift, calm yourself, and turn critical tones into loving, inquisitive statements.

Before beginning, get primed by looking back at your turnarounds from Remedy 2. Say them to yourself silently or out loud. Vary your pitch, cadence, and volume. Then, reflect upon a few examples from your life. You can write the name of someone who speaks/spoke kindly to you, how you might talk to an injured child, or speak to a frightened pet. Then, let your inner voice mimic the appropriate cadence, tone, and volume.

As you encounter self-talk or find yourself ruminating, consider how you might hold your body or hands, relax your jaw, and modulate your breathing to assure yourself you're on your own team. How might you use your inner voice to motivate yourself? In what way can you shift your voice when you phrase a question to convey genuine curiosity that will generate helpful insight rather than beat yourself up? Over the next several days, journal here about the process and any insights that come to mind.

_____

_____

_____

"The voice of the sea speaks to the soul."
—*Kate Chopin* (1850–1904)

What if your inner voice spoke to you like that—steady, rhythmic, and alive with life?

Remedy 5

Who's That You're Talking To?

Initial Notes

Now that you're noticing and really hearing the content of your thoughts, as well as working with the tone and other paralanguage features, let's add a shout out—*to yourself*.

Having suffered anxiety from a young age, I learned early on how to talk myself down from what-if bridges and catastrophized despair. What worked? Saying my name. "*Come on, Sheri. This is nothing. Just breathe.*" Referring to myself by name in my thoughts has successfully seen me through everything from a rape at knifepoint at age 18 to appearing on radio and TV. So, it was no surprise to me to learn that introspection researchers have found using one's own name helps.[1,2] Saying your own name in your thoughts is more generally known as "illeism." It might seem weird at first, but using your own name engages what's known as "psychological distancing," which we'll talk about more later in the book. In essence, by using your name, you step back from your emotions and respond instead like you might to another person in distress.

Next time you find yourself in a negative thought loop, and your mind won't shut off, try referring to yourself by name: "*Sheri, it's time to let this go. Your mind wants to solve this, but you know there's not much you can do tonight.*" I sometimes then take a second distancing step, personifying my own mind and talking to it. "*Thank you, Mind. Thank you for all you do for me. And, for tonight, it's okay to rest.*"

Of course, you'll use your own name and whatever phrases make sense for you.

Why This Remedy Works

Using your own name when talking to yourself is part of a broader technique of emotional distancing. Such distancing causes your brain to process the information less personally. It's like becoming an outsider in your own life. Your emotions are calmer than when you refer to yourself as "I." So, you're less affected.

How to Use This Remedy

The task at hand is to purposely refer to yourself by name. Start with easy stuff. At a restaurant, think, *Well, Sue, what looks good on this menu?* Or, when you've been hard at work on something for a while, think, *Dee, it's time to take a break and go get some steps.* By using your name as you purposely think about everyday routines, you'll begin to form a habit. That way, when you're facing emotionally wrought moments and anguished rumination, you'll lean more naturally on this technique. In addition to habitually using your name for routine events, expand the practice into other situations. Say your name during inner pep talks (which I recommend) or whenever you're stressed.

As you engage in healthy self-talk and refer to yourself by name, notice how you feel. Does your mood shift? Does the content of your thoughts change? Reflect on your experiences here.

_____

_____

_____

_____

_____

_____

_____

_____

"Elizabeth, be firm with yourself ..."
—*from the journal of Elizabeth Barrett Browning (1806–1861).*

"Mary Ann, remember what you are capable of ..."
—*from the journal of Mary Ann Evans (1819–1880).*
Her novels were written under the male pseudonym George Eliot.

Remedy 6

Wee-Hour Check-in

Initial Notes

Awakened from a dead sleep, you punch your pillow and roll over, praying that this time you can drift back into peaceful slumber. Too bad your mind has other plans. It's already stewing.

Traumatic events and ongoing stress can keep us chained to worrisome thoughts. Our nervous system gets triggered, our bodies release stress hormones including cortisol, and we switch into fight-or-flight mode. The way our brains naturally respond to stress tamps down our awareness of physical needs.[1] That makes sense when we're in immediate danger and can't safely stop for a bio-break or we might get eaten by a tiger. But when under attack by ongoing stress and heartache, the tendency to become unaware or dismissive of interoceptive signals, the body's internal cues like hunger or fatigue, magnifies situational worries and can perhaps cause physical harm. Our bodies need rest, and impaired sleep can lead to impaired health.

I mainly work with life coaching clients who are over 60 and affected by ambiguous loss and other major life changes. When they tell me they wake up to painful rumination in the night, they attribute the sleeplessness to their stress. However, that's frequently only partially true. My first question is whether awakening in the wee hours is something new. More than half of them will think for a minute and then say they quite often used to arise in the night to pee. When asked if they still need to do that, most reply in the affirmative, but say they usually don't realize that at first. Instead, they lie there awhile, entombed in a bed of anguish until, minutes to hours later, they realize they need to go.

Sometimes, we stir in the night, and our minds shift into high gear before we're even fully awake. And then we lie there, trapped by our burdensome thoughts. Especially when we're stressed, or when we've experienced so much stress that our nervous system maintains a low-grade state of alarm, a similar disconnection to physical needs happens during waking hours. The remedy? To train ourselves to intentionally check in with our physical needs.

Why This Remedy Works

Trauma and ongoing stress can compromise our "felt experience."[1] Our brains naturally inhibit interoceptive signals pertaining to our physical needs in order to prioritize danger and the need to act fast. It's a survival mechanism that, in the face of ongoing mental and emotional distress, doesn't always serve us well.

How to Use This Remedy

Your task is to notice when your thinking dips into negativity or circles the looping drain of rumination—and immediately check in with your physical self. Whether in the wee hours, after sitting for long work periods, or while in the zone of a much-loved hobby, be aware when any anxious thinking intrudes. Then, intentionally ask yourself what your body might need. Are you hungry or tired? Do you need to use the bathroom? Are your legs falling asleep?

Just as people awaken in the night needing to use the bathroom, but the urge gets sidelined by despairing thoughts—even though the physical need may be what roused them—this happens during wakeful hours, too. Hunger or thirst, for example, rouses you from your pastime or work. Yet, when stressed, you may not be immediately cognizant of your physical need. Here, you're practicing becoming more aware of your whole self, mind *and* body. You might thank your physical body for shaking you out of your head. Honor your physical self. Give your body what it needs.

Journal here about your experiences as you pay more attention to your physical self. How do the needs or sensations relate to any rumination and stressed inner dialogue? Note what your body needed, how you responded, and any results.

_____

_____

_____

REMEDY 6: Wee-Hour Check-in

Remedy 7

Shift into Neutral

Initial Notes

While we're physically in the here and now, we're very often mentally somewhere else. This is called "Mental Time Travel" (MTT).[1] We use our episodic memory to draw from the past. Or we imagine possible scenarios in the future.

Rumination, by its nature, projects us forward to catastrophized imaginal futures or backward to upsetting scenes. Overthinkers know all too well that MTT can be a curse. We don't choose to relive the stress of painful interactions and disappointing events. Yet off the mind goes, shuffling down agonizing byways. Or we travel forward to a distant tomorrow where every imagined bleak scenario is realized times ten.

Even *good* memories can become painful if we look wistfully back to a time that, with distance, appears kinder and simpler. The gnawing ache of loss over all that has changed triggers distress. We pine for what once was and regret what we now believe we didn't fully appreciate while we had the chance.

Rumination leaves us feeling powerless, unable to shut off, and in distress. But MTT, when focused on specific, constructive tasks, has positive benefits. For that reason, we'll ease into a basic, deliberate practice.

Why This Remedy Works

What and how we think about the past or future can negatively impact our feelings about our current lives as well as harm our physical and mental well-being.[2] Bracing for a future we've built up as catastrophic amps up stress. When the past gains a gilded glow, the present can pale in comparison. As prescribed below, a basic and neutral use of MTT quells intruding thoughts and gives the brain something helpful to focus on, which calms anxiety and can increase happiness.[3]

How to Use This Remedy

This week, whenever you find your mind wandering, you will exercise your planning faculties. The aim is to keep this very simple. Here's how: If troubled thoughts keep you awake at night, travel briskly in time to the day ahead. Deliberatively focus on your routines: *bathing, eating, driving....* To break free of a waking episode of negative thinking, purposely shift toward planning whatever's next: *finishing a project, a trip to the grocery store, clocking out of work....* In every practice, give yourself the gift of your own presence. Close your eyes and take your time as you fully immerse yourself, mentally, in these imagined routines of your immediate future.

To acquire this new habit more easily, consider coming up with sentence prompts you can remember and rely upon to move into short-term planning mode. Here, I've included some simple examples that capture the mundane nature of neutral MTT. Remember, we're discarding extremes.

- Next (or tomorrow) I need to . . .
- Then I will . . .
- I'm going to get in my car, turn the key in the ignition, and drive to ...
- I will stop by my coworker's desk to say goodbye ...
- When I get home I will ...

Over the next week or so, experiment with brief forays into neutral MTT even when you're not in a negative thought loop. The practice becomes routine, training your brain to use this mental superpower for improved focus and to stay on track.

Use the space on the next pages to journal about your continued experiences using neutral MTT. Did you find yourself resistant to the idea or practice? Did your focus and viewpoint change as you experimented? Are you averse to planning? Did the planning come naturally to you? How often did you find yourself in a ruminative loop? Write out whatever comes to mind. Any insights become personal gains, gems you can draw strength from in the present and build upon in the future.

Remedy 8

The Shake Break

Initial Notes

There's something to the message made famous by singer Taylor Swift in her hit "Shake It Off." As a dog lover, I've seen them vigorously shake off after a stressful encounter, a scare, or even rough buddy play. Other animals also exhibit this innate shaking or trembling behavior that dispels stress and restores nervous system balance. You can do this, too.

Why This Remedy Works

Therapeutic approaches, including Peter Levine's Somatic Experiencing (SE) and David Berceli's Trauma Release Exercises (TRE), provide a basis for this remedy. When your out-of-control mind hijacks your nervous system, you can borrow from the animal world just as these trauma experts' processes do. Purposely changing physical position to shake out the body works to disrupt your thoughts, which we'll talk about more in Remedy 9. The movement itself can lift mood and reduce anxiety, thereby calming spinning thoughts.[1]

 How to Use This Remedy

If possible, stand up and literally shake out your body. I suggest you begin with your hands, arms, legs, and then your whole body. Continue for 30 seconds up to a few minutes.

If you must remain seated or reclined, alter your movements to shake yourself out as best you can. Quickly pump your fists at your sides, for example. Shake out your hands from the wrists. Lift your arms and shake them. Wriggle your feet. Bump your legs up and down. You might try lifting and lowering your shoulders repeatedly in quick succession. Do what it takes to make this exercise work. Even at a desk in a shared workspace, you can discreetly lift and lower your legs, then wriggle your feet, and pump your fists.

Don't wait until you're in a static haze of emotional thinking. Now that you're more aware of your thinking patterns, you are primed to notice bodily tension cues as well. Commuting in traffic? Take a shake break whenever momentarily stopped and then after you've safely arrived. Have a lot to get done, a series of stressful errands, or difficult conversations? Take periodic shake breaks to dispel tension as you go.

Notice your bodily sensations after your shake breaks. Warm? Tingly? Lighter? Also notice your mind's shifts. Do you feel more at ease? Reflect on the experience.

Remedy 9

Pattern Interrupt

Initial Notes

Skilled YouTubers know the power of surprise. A rubber chicken flies across the screen, a fire alarm sounds, or a silly character appears to tell a quick joke. The video makers capture and recapture viewers' attention with what's called a "pattern interrupt." The technique is also used in sales to interrupt prospects' automatic "not interested" response and by skilled persuaders in other interpersonal interactions. Disrupting a pattern stalls automatic behavior or thinking and displaces whatever usually comes next. As experienced ruminators, we can use the same concept to interrupt our thinking and add something new and helpful.

Rubber chickens, fire alarms, or silly characters aside, imagine your negative thought loops like a video reel. On and on they go, one *what-if*, *I-wish*, or *if-only* leading to another and another. It's exhausting. What can you insert to disrupt the pattern?

Why This Remedy Works

Rumination exacerbates depression and a range of other mental disorders, as well as contributes to behaviors such as substance abuse and binge eating, which are associated with adverse health outcomes. Disrupting the cascade of thoughts that lead into and sustain negative rumination affords a pause in which to switch to a helpful mitigating action. A 2023 study using a "just in time" intervention revealed that the good results lasted.[1]

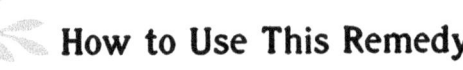

How to Use This Remedy

This remedy leans on your foundational first few weeks with this workbook. Now that you're more quickly aware when your thoughts dip into negativity, you'll be prepared to intervene. Come up with some pattern interrupt ideas you can easily implement. I've listed a few ideas below. Circle ones you'll try, and write a few of your own.

- Tap the top of your head with your fingertips
- Stamp your feet on the floor
- Keep a notepad handy and write a dollar sign, exclamation mark, or other symbol
- Get up from your chair and stretch
- Drink water
- Wear a soft elastic band around your wrist and snap it
- Pet a pet
- Stroke soft fabric such as velvet

_____

_____

_____

_____

_____

_____

_____

Once you've done the decided-upon action, you'll need to use the "Your Turnaround" technique in Remedy 2. By now, you're getting a pretty good idea of what sorts of events prompt your rumination as well as its tone. You might want to review your relevant notes from earlier weeks. And then come up with more turnarounds here. The idea is to make these second nature. To that end, I've added a few more generic turnarounds below—this time without the negative thought prompts. Read through these examples, preferably out loud, and reflect upon the prominent features of your own negativity. As you do, consider when these phrases, or variations, might work for you. Write out new phrases, as well as any thoughts of when they might be helpful for you. As in my examples, use second person (you) language to add beneficial emotional distance.

- You've risen to challenges before. You can do that again now.
- Your best is good enough.
- That was yesterday. This is a new day.
- You've got this!
- This feeling, like this moment, is temporary.
- Other adults can take care of their feelings.

_____

_____

_____

_____

_____

_____

_____

_____

Over the course of the next week or so, practice one or more pattern interrupts (trying several is a good idea), and then use your inner voice wisely. State a useful turnaround phrase that fits. You can also add another technique, such as the neutral MTT of basic planning from Remedy 7, *Shift into Neutral*. Keep notes about using pattern interrupts. Which were easy to implement? Did you run into any snags? Write about your thoughts shifting to wiser ground. Is this becoming more natural? Did you add another tactic? What worked well for you? What can you learn from any challenge you faced in doing this exercise?

"Hold the thought of what you want, not of what you fear."
—*Annie Rix Militz* (1856–1924)

Remedy 10

Cherished Evidence

Initial Notes

A friend of mine moved across the country and, within a year, lost her sweet young adult child and a beloved dog. Both died rather suddenly, and her days grew dim. Yet, she filled her social media pages with photographs of happier times. Cherishing those special moments, not only with her dog and child, but with other people and places she loved, helped her cope. By remembering the good times, she reminded herself that her life had been fun, and that it could be again.

When we're stressed, grieving, or in shock, our thinking can be so dark that it's tough to remember our lives holding any light. Savoring good memories interrupts negative thoughts and can make us feel happier.[1]

By engaging in activities that require our full attention, we shift naturally to here-and-now. We interact with our physical world and those around us. Adopting a habit of being fully present makes us good company for ourselves and others.

Seeing my friend's photographic evidence of her love for people, pets, and places in her past and present has inspired me to take more photos. While she still occasionally posts about her losses, her social media shares are mostly about the current life she continues to treasure. Her many photos are a bank of cherished evidence, proof of her happiness.

Why This Remedy Works

The purpose of this remedy is twofold. Savoring good moments helps us feel better and gain perspective on the temporal nature of current troubles or our sadness while enduring them.

Mindful activities, such as photography, divert attention away from negative inner dialogue and immerse us in the present.

How to Use This Remedy

This week, make a conscious effort to take digital photos of everything you do and see that interests you or brings you joy. Include other people in the pictures when you're enjoying their company. Get silly candid shots and have them "cheese" for the camera. What sparks your interest in your surroundings? Look for something. Are your roses blooming? Get pics. Are the birds at the feeder? Take photos. Are the dandelions going to seed? They look quite beautiful if you lie in the grass for up-close photographs. Fallen leaves, the sparkle of sunlight on water, a bright umbrella, the clouds above.... Notice the beauty around you, immerse yourself, and capture it. Don't let a day go by without taking pictures. And while immersed, don't bother with editing them.

Then, when thoughts turn to wishes and what-ifs, pull out your phone and scroll through those recent pics. As you look at the images, relax your body with a few easy breaths and take your time viewing the pictures (and perhaps removing duplicates). Notice any details you may have missed in the moment. Is that a tiny insect in the photo? Is your neighbor struggling to contain her uber friendly dog? Congratulate yourself on your creativity. Marvel at a captured scene's beauty, and giggle at a silly or awkward shot. Bring to your mind and savor any scents, sounds, or snippets of conversation you can recall. You *do* have fun sometimes, people *do* like you, and there *is* beauty and joy in your world. Plus, as you learned in Remedy 9, flipping through photographs is a disruptor.

You can also disrupt rumination by pulling out older photographs and perusing your more distant past. If you're inclined, posting photos to social media can be fun. Think of interesting captions or funny sayings to go with them. You may be surprised at the comments you receive. At the very least, you can scroll through those postings later and marvel at your clever words (while also enjoying the photos again).

Every day this week, write about what it was like to take so many photographs, to look through them, and to study your world from this new vantage point. How do the photos make you feel? Did you enjoy staying alert for something to photograph? What was the act of noticing details like for you—both while taking the pictures and while viewing them later? What did you enjoy most about the process?

Remedy 11

Message to Self— Chill Out

Initial Notes
You may have seen athletes or social media influencers gleefully sinking into an icy bath. They smile as their lips turn blue and discuss all sorts of known health benefits including stress relief and improved mood. Even so, the thought of plunging into cold water gives me chills. You too? Then you'll be glad to learn that exposing just a few inches of skin to cold can be good for you. Here, we'll strip down to the bare minimum for cold exposure benefits without the shivers.

Why This Remedy Works
Lower heart rate and higher heart rate variability are evidence of nervous system calming. Cold that's targeted to a small area to stimulate the vagus nerve can bring these effects. The vagus nerve works like an information highway where signals travel both ways between the heart (and other organs) and the brain. Targeted cold sends a clear message to self: *Chill out*.

 ## How to Use This Remedy
Place an ice cube or a small ice pack against the side of your neck, covering with cloth as needed. A 2018 study measured beneficial change after just 16 seconds when the "posterior triangle," the right neck area just above the clavicle, was targeted.[1] So, there is no need for long, drawn-out cold sessions. Let your comfort be your guide.

Try this exercise for acute moments when your mind won't settle. Also chill out regularly to test this tool and your response to it when your mind isn't so wound up. Try cold exposure on five consecutive nights or just after lunch every weekday, for example. If you want to, listen to soothing music or sit outdoors to enjoy the sounds of nature while you practice this remedy.

However you choose to "chill out," be sure to journal about your experience. Did you note the calming effect on your mind? Your body? Were you calm and cool? Whatever you notice, take time to write and reflect.

Remedy 12

Learning Curve, A Five-Star Review

Initial Notes

In the first *Learning Curve*, you learned about the *why* that motivates your energetic fire to work at willful, positive change: your "Wi-Fi." You deepened your commitment to yourself and these processes—and here you are! Good for you. You've completed many more remedies and have reached another *Learning Curve*.

Why Reviewing Works

Reviewing previously learned material provides new opportunities to relate, process, and grow. You aren't a static bot functioning at the same level and with the same information as you navigate through life. Experiences teach and change you, so you relate to what you've learned in new ways. This broadens perspectives and understanding.

Reviewing aids automated recall so you connect what techniques fit with which ruminative content and, over time and with practice, rely on them without effort. This "recall fluency" helps you make what you learn your own and helps you adapt in real time as you go about living.[1]

Measure Your Progress

Of the skills covered in Remedies 4–11, which have you experimented with? Below, you'll find each of the techniques listed along with an explanatory line intended to jog your memory. To the left, check off (or draw a star) next to each of the techniques you've tried.

Take some time to review your notes from, and reflect again upon, each experience. Run through the steps again if that feels necessary. Then, using a scale of 0-10 where ten means super helpful and zero means not helpful all, write the number that best represents your experience with each technique (on the line to the right).

_____ **4: Watch Your Tone** *(Identify and improve how you talk to yourself.)* _____

_____ **5: Who's That You're Talking To?** *(Name yourself in your thoughts.)* _____

_____ **6: Wee-Hour Check-In** *(Notice your physical feelings.)* _____

_____ **7: Shift into Neutral** *(Refocus on basic plans for the immediate future.)* _____

_____ **8: The Shake Break** *(Expel excess energy by shaking it off.)* _____

_____ **9: Pattern Interrupt** *(Disrupt negative thinking with something new.)* _____

_____ **10: Cherished Evidence** *(Immerse in the present and later savor.)* _____

_____ **11: Chill Out** *(Calm your nervous system by applying cold.)* _____

Catch Up or Toss

Did you skip any of the techniques entirely? Or, do you feel you didn't give some techniques adequate effort? Now is the time to go back and try any skipped remedies or experiment with ones you believe warrant additional time and exploration. Jot the names down below and then use the lines with the specific remedies to record your progress. Add your ratings above. No matter where you fall in terms of completion, be sure to celebrate your efforts.

_____

_____

_____

_____

What Didn't Help?

We are all individuals with unique circumstances, histories, likes, and dislikes. What works for one person may not be helpful to another. Using your ratings above, consider any remedies you may have found *un*helpful.

Take a few minutes to review and reflect upon what didn't resonate and why. As you reflect, notice any physical responses such as tense muscles, upset stomach, or racing heartbeat, as well as any thoughts that accompany the sensations. Such awareness can provide you with useful insight into your reactions and possible resistance. Perhaps a particular exercise pricks at a tender history that warrants further exploration or that you simply acknowledge and, in so doing, honor yourself. It's up to you whether digging in is appropriate or necessary right now.

Allow yourself to stop and do further journaling, seek the compassionate ear of a trusted friend or clinician, or to simply bid farewell to any tools so far that don't resonate. This workbook is designed to help you identify what works—and part of that includes knowing what doesn't. Use the lines below to write out, honestly, how you feel and what comes to mind when you consider what didn't resonate.

_____

_____

_____

_____

_____

_____

_____

_____

Make the Remedies Your Own

Remedies 1, 2, and 4 had *Additional Tips and Techniques* sections. This is a good time to revisit those sections. Perhaps you have already worked with these to better understand yourself and make the exercises best fit your needs. If so, consider what was important. To gain insight that can help you as you work forward, write about those here. What changes did you make? Why did you make these choices? What insights did you gain? Reflect and journal about these now.

Favorites So Far

Using your ratings of the techniques covered in Remedies 4–11, note the tools you found most helpful. Don't worry so much about the scores themselves. Just note the highest ones. Consider why these worked for you as well as they did. What did you like about them? How easy were they to implement and remember?

Record your thoughts on the lines below. These reflections will help you to identify *your* most fruitful times for experimenting with the techniques. You'll also gain insight into how you might begin to make the exercises more your own so they can best fit your lifestyle and your thinking habits. After journaling about these, use the last block of lines in this *Learning Curve* to record the titles of your favorites so far. You're building a "go-to list" of tools that best works for you.

_____

_____

_____

_____

_____

_____

_____

_____

_____

_____

My Go-Tos

Remedy 13

Making Tomorrow Real

Initial Notes

A long time ago, my husband Brian and I visited a couple in their early 80s we didn't frequently see. They'd aged a lot. The wife had quit coloring her once-natural fiery red curls and now sported a stark white pixie cut. She gripped a cane but got around well in the fashion-savvy orthotic slippers she'd bought off the TV. As we left, the husband stopped where the padded carpeting met adjacent tile-floor. "Sorry, I can't walk you all the way to door," he said, explaining that the hard floor hurt his feet.

In my forties then, I remember asking my husband if we were going to get like them one day. I just couldn't imagine it. Me with white hair? A snowy cap, needing a cane, or feet always in pain weren't on my radar.

Nine years my senior, Brian must have had a slightly better grasp on the reality of aging. "Oh, no," he said with a chuckle. "Not us."

The difficulty in imagining oneself growing old isn't unique to me. Neuroimaging research has shown that, when imagining our future selves, the brain reacts similarly to when we think about strangers.[1] So, how can we take sound steps for the future now when we don't even know that future person we're supposed to become?

This remedy helps bridge the gap to your future self. The best use of your time and energy will come into sharper focus. So, you'll be more motivated to drop rumination loops that get you nowhere.

Why This Remedy Works

People frequently tell me they wasted much of their lives chasing another person or dream that was beyond their control. They regret wasting so much time. You can benefit from their hindsight via temporal distancing with its emotional padding and decreased distress.[2, 3, 4] How you feel about your current circumstances is not the same as how you'll feel in the future. Also, this remedy clarifies the finite nature of our lives, which triggers urgency—and wiser choices now.[1, 6]

How to Use This Remedy

This week's task has three easy steps.

First, look at old photos of yourself. Start with your earliest ages until now. Just looking at the photos can suffice. However, if you're inclined, you could organize a timeline with physical or digital photos you order by year.

The second step is to get in mind a clearer picture of your future self. If you can, study photographs of relatives in old age. Then think about how your own face and body might change. If you feel comfortable uploading your photos, use an AI age progression tool to make the changes more real. A phone or online app works. Or, upload a current photo to an AI program such as ChatGPT and ask it to create age progression images for two, five, or ten years into the future.

Third, with a clearer image of your maturing self, imagine what you'll be doing in the next years or decade. One of my clients in her early sixties said she was making all her decisions now for the 85-year-old she was to become. For the first time in her life, she was thinking into the distant future, trying to picture herself realistically in old age, and acting to safeguard her future self. This included career choices, relationship shifts, building her savings, and planning where she'd live. She also stopped ruminating about what she realized she had no control over or wasn't so important to her future.

On the lines below, journal about several time blocks in your future life. One, five, or ten years, for example. Whatever makes sense for you. Record your decided-upon future age at the start of each block, and then fully immerse yourself in visualizing your future. How do you plan to spend your time? What will you think about? Who and what are important to your future self at the projected ages?

Once you've looked into your future realistically, reflect upon what's most important to you now. What decisions can you make to support your future? Does ruminating waste your life? Journal about this.

Note: Ageism can be so deeply embedded in language and culture that we aren't always consciously aware of its presence. Yet, its effects are felt and internalized. This is unfortunate because negative, ageist stereotypes such as older people being inflexible, bumbling, sick, cognitively impaired, frail, and boring are largely myths.[6] Are your feelings based on fears or negativity about growing older? Journal about these feelings. Then seek out healthy examples to aspire to, whether celebrities, historical figures (both public and private), or people in your immediate life. Make decisions now that support your future self.

 Additional Tips and Techniques

For some people, considering what they've learned about life over the years helps them to put into perspective what's important now. As you look at photos of yourself from early ages onward, what do you wish a younger you would have known? Consider what was important to you at one point in your life that you later realized wasn't worth so much focus. Write a letter to your younger self about your thoughts. Or, forget the letter and just journal what comes to mind.

_____

_____

_____

_____

_____

_____

_____

_____

_____

"The wise woman looks ahead.
She does not waste her time dreaming of the impossible,
but plans for the probable and prepares for the possible."
—*Margaret E. Sangster, poet, essayist and magazine editor* (1838–1912)

Remedy 14

N-E-W

Initial Notes

I like meaningful acronyms and frequently invent them. These easily recalled reminders help to break habits, shift gears, or move you to action. The best ones use a familiar acronym in a new way or spell out a related healing word or phrase. Here are two I've come up with previously and used in a book or with groups:

PB&J. Many will recognize the acronym for peanut butter and jelly, but I use it to help people who are overwhelmed. P-rioritize, B-reak into manageable tasks, and J-ust leave it. Even when you're overwhelmed, if you prioritize tasks, break them into bite-sized chunks, and make the decision to just leave some tasks entirely, you can see a way through the muck.

SEAL. To achieve a goal requires breaking old habits and embracing better ones. SEAL helps you to identify needed changes and handshake on it—with yourself. S-ubstitute, E-nhance, A-dapt, L-eave off. Under each word, list items needed to achieve the desired change. What better habits can you substitute for less effective ones? What strengths can you enhance? How will you need to adapt? And what must you leave off doing altogether? *SEAL the deal!*

This remedy's title is an acronym specific to ruminative thinking. *NEW*: N-otice the negativity, E-xtinguish it, and take a new W-ay forward. I sometimes tell clients to come up with visual imagery such as a spotlight, a fire extinguisher, and a sign that points to an entrance to a hopeful new path.

For a runaway brain that twists and turns down ever-darkening paths, an invented acronym can help you hit the brakes and steer up and out of the maze.

Why This Remedy Works

A lovely picnic can be ruined by ants. So can a peaceful mind. In the 1960s, psychologist Aaron Beck (one of the founders of cognitive behavioral therapy) used the acronym ANTS for pesky A-utomatic N-egative T-houghts. Runaway thinking is no picnic and Beck's ANTS clarifies how a simple acronym can help you recognize unwelcome, habitual, negative thoughts and brush them away.

How to Use This Remedy

This Remedy has two steps—and it's fun! So, get into a quiet space, take a deep breath, and exhale slowly. Let your imagination be your guide as you tackle the first step and create your own acronyms. Use this remedy's title (N-E-W), my PB&J and SEAL examples, and Beck's ANTS as launch points for your own creative energy. Don't fret over not-good-enough or this-is-dumb ANTS. Brush those Automatic Negative Thoughts aside. Allow yourself to freely brainstorm words or phrases for acronyms that are uniquely meaningful to you and your negative thought patterns. Feel free to cross out some ideas and start anew as needed. Choose a funny, sarcastic, or hopeful tone, and switch as the mood strikes. It's okay to vent a little or laugh as you work.

Once you've come up with a few that make sense to you, the second step is to use them. Any time your thoughts dip into negativity or painful repetition, Notice, Extinguish, and find a new Way forward (as an example). You'll use your own acronyms, whatever they are. Write about the experience as the week moves forward.

Additional Tips and Techniques

> Not vibing with the creative part? Borrow from the acronym examples provided here. Alter them as you see fit. You might also draw from or borrow some of the sayings mentors in your life have used.

_____

_____

_____

_____

Remedy 15

You're Here Now, and Safe

Initial Notes

One early spring, as winter's dismal veil lifted to sunshine and blooms, my husband came down with shingles. Talk about a miserable month. The extensive, angry rash and pain he described as electric shocks were horrific. I was worried, of course, and mentioned the illness to a few other people. Each time brought groans and stories of their own or a loved one's equally grisly or even worse experience. The wretched nature of shingles aside, it's the way you contract it that's of interest here.

In anyone who ever had chicken pox, the virus remains and lurks, sleeping sometimes for decades, until triggered as shingles. That's how our emotional woundings can be. Going along just fine—and *pow*—the mind goes tumbling into sadness and pain.

When we're triggered by something—an event, the time of year, something we're told or that we see—and then immerse ourselves in old hurt via mental time travel, we resurrect the hurt like a painful rash. To work through and process our emotions about past events requires a bit of time, energy, and patience. For now, let's pause and fully immerse ourselves *in the present*.

Note: In this remedy, I've talked about getting emotionally and cognitively lost in incidents and issues from the past, but immersing in the present also inoculates us against current or future-based anxiety and overthinking. So, whether it's regret from yesteryear, the replaying of today's tense conversation, worry over next month's big event, or when there's no definitive time stamp to uncertainty and dread, this remedy applies.

Why This Remedy Works

When triggered, your physiological stress response readies your body to fight or flee. That's great if there's a real danger, but not when the danger is in your mind, as in thinking of a past experience or a future worry. The techniques described below are examples of "grounding." The act of grounding pulls your attention out of your whirling mind and into your body, or out of the past or future into the present. *You're here now, and safe.*

To experience how this works, imagine your thoughts as a wild jungle monkey, swinging from tree to tree. See the monkey leaping and chattering and climbing. . . Now, imagine the monkey dropping to the ground and standing still. A serene expression falls over his face. His tail rests gently on the ground. His feet are planted solidly in the dirt. His arms rest at his sides. As he stands there, still and steady, a gentle breeze ruffles his fur.

See how your attention shifted? You were in the present, focusing on the monkey. That's how it feels to *ground*.

How to Use This Remedy

Below, I'll describe several grounding exercises. They're derived from well-known techniques that have been adopted, titled, and altered by me and countless others. You may, over time, alter these to fit your own needs. For this remedy, your task is to practice them. Choose one for any episodes of negative thinking, but even if your mind is calm, try out the techniques. Grounding is a form of mindfulness that helps when needed—and can bring lasting benefits. Knowing how to and practicing presence means living life as it unfolds, immersed in and appreciating every precious moment.

You can try these exercises in any order. Use each one more than once, at different times of day or night, and under different circumstances. Don't hurry. Take two days to two weeks as you experiment with the variations. Later, write about how grounding helped in general over the days or week(s) as well as for each exercise. I've included lines after each one, as well as space at the end of this remedy.

TECHNIQUE: Sensory Cone

You can do this exercise anywhere. Inside or outside, in any room or space. The aim is to take your time, say three to six minutes, but in a pinch, even a swift, abbreviated practice can help.

Start by placing one or both hands gently over your heart. Take a few long, slow breaths in through the nose and out through the mouth. Then, continue to breathe easily throughout this exercise. In ... and out ... gently.

Now, engage the senses. Start with five items you can see and decrease by one item for each of the primary five senses.

Seeing (five things you see): Take your time to look at your nearby surroundings. As your vision falls upon what's nearby or in the room, you'll name five things within a phrase. *Example*: The metal slats of the bench are supporting me. A small gray bird is pecking at the crumbs on the ground. There's an emblem that names the company that laid this slab of concrete. The wooden post supports the small tree. A yellow dandelion is blooming in the grass.

Feeling (four things you can feel): Settle into your body and notice what you feel. *Example*: The breeze is ruffling my hair against my cheek. My stomach feels full. I notice the pinch of my shoelaces on the top of my foot. The sunlight is warm on my shoulders.

Hearing (three things you can hear): Listen to the sounds around you. *Example*: The birds in the tree are chirping. I can hear their wings flutter as they fly in at the feeder. Out near the street, a leaf blower revs.

Smelling (two things you can smell): Smells aren't always a strong presence. If you can't access two scents in your immediate vicinity, feel free to recall scents you enjoy. *Example*: Lifting my hand close to my face, I detect the soft scent of soap. I love the way the food in the crockpot smells when it's nearing dinnertime.

Tasting (one thing you can taste): Taste what's already present, what you imagine, or the sip of a drink or something else that's handy. This might be the coffee you sip or can still taste in your mouth. The minty flavor of gum or the sharp bite of tangy cheese in your sandwich. The spiced eggnog you look forward to in the winter. *Example*: I can still taste maple syrup from this morning's waffle.

Variations:

- If decreasing the number is bothersome or takes too much energy, just choose a few items for each sense without counting.

  Note: As you repeat this technique, notice which sense you lean upon. Perhaps your focus is frequently on how you feel in your body, or you enjoy lovely scents. These tendencies provide clues for interests to explore or to validate your feelings in some way. For example, I love the different sounds birds' wings make. When sitting quietly where they're landing, I can identify a house finch from an oak titmouse by their unique wing beats. What does this mean for me? That I feel connected to birds and am calmed by their presence. Also, noise tires me. My ears crave the soothing balm of nature.

- Even focusing on one or two of the senses helps ground you in the present moment. Most people find using their sight comes easiest. If you're pressed for time or have an urgent need to ground quickly, try closing your eyes and listening, feeling, or smelling. Name as much as you can in a single moment or while you wash your hands, fix your coffee, or wait on hold or in a line. Or, simply touch something tactile in your environment. I like to pet my sweet lapdog, Ginger. You might choose to stroke plush velvet, run your fingertip over a ring you wear, and notice the subtle texture of the stones, their settings, and the metal band. The trick is to give your full attention.

TECHNIQUE: Here S/he Is Now

This technique involves immersing yourself in the moment and narrating the here-and-now experience in the third-person. Here's an example:

Sheri McGregor sits with Gingersnap's fuzzy warmth beside her. In Sheri's lap is her Vibes Up! brand Tree Hugger pillow which supports the laptop she's using to type. Outside, a woodpecker knocks at the tree, and the twisty call of hummingbirds lifts above the sage blooms near the house that Sheri sees in her mind's eye. Across the room, the sound of trickling water from the aquarium's filter catches Sheri's attention, a gentle reminder that it's time to refill the tank. Sunlight slants in on the foot-long canoe-shaped leaves of the Red Congo philodendron that stretches toward the window. Beyond the glass, a tiny oak titmouse flutters in and lands on the deck rail. It cocks its head this way and that, its head crest flattening back as it leans forward, eyeing the water dish on the deck. Sheri notices her shoulders are aching. Time to put her work down and move her body.

Variations:

- Choose someone else who is nearby, imagine what they see and feel as they take in the surroundings. Imagine inhabiting that person's space, see from their eyes, and feel what they may be feeling. Narrate from their perspective.

- Devoted pets are usually very attuned to our energy and movement. If you have a pet close, imagine inhabiting your pet's space and being next to you. Narrate from the pet's perspective, perhaps including how they see and experience your own breathing, mood, and physical stance.

_____

_____

_____

_____

_____

_____

_____

TECHNIQUE: Move

The title says it all. You can choose to flex your wrists, wriggle your fingers or toes, raise your arms over your head ... Or do something that encompasses your whole body, such as standing up and shaking yourself around or going outside for a stroll. As you twist or wriggle or shake or stroll, be aware of the movements and how your body feels while making them. Notice your hips in their sockets as you walk. Be aware of each finger wriggling. Does anything creak or hurt? Are you grateful for the mobility?

_____

_____

_____

_____

_____

_____

_____

As you experiment with these grounding techniques over the next several days, take additional notes. How does getting grounded help?

_____

_____

_____

_____

My Notes

Remedy 16

Awestruck

Initial Notes

When we moved from dry Southern California to the rainier Sierra foothills, we were amazed by the variety of wildlife. Dragonflies swarmed in the air and smaller nymphs rested on the ground and in the bushes near the house. When we put in a small pond at the front of our house, the varieties proliferated.

Some dragonflies have spotted wings reminiscent of checkered racing flags. Others are big and bright red, pale or neon blue, dull gray, or small. The longer we've lived here the more types we see. And they've provided a distraction during some intense periods of chaos involving a family member's mental illness (when rumination can reign).

One hot summer morning during a particularly troubling period, I noticed a thick black dragonfly carrying something on either side of its back. *What was that?* Immediately engaged, my imagination sparked with possibilities. I shielded my eyes against the sun as the swift insect jetted near and then away. Were those black packages it carried its babies? Food? Some strange survival adaptation? From what I knew of dragonflies, nothing made sense.

Over the next few weeks, more of this variety appeared, none ever landing long enough for me to get a good look. Finally, I resorted to research and discovered its fitting name: *Saddlebags*. Only, those weren't saddlebags at all. Just shiny black splotches on its transparent wings. An optical illusion which, in flight, looked like saddlebags. I laughed at myself, shared the news with my husband, and turned my attention to the next natural wonder in our rural neighborhood.

What I experienced was awe, elicited from the presence of nature, which has been shown in repeated studies to mitigate mood and deliver us from the troubles we can't solve. Getting awestruck by nature isn't dependent on grand landscapes, vast oceans, or majestic mountains either. As my dragonfly story illustrates, even an insect can carry the gift of deliverance.

Why This Remedy Works

People tend to dismiss the powerful well-being effects of nature.[1] This remedy's task is to get near nature wherever you find it. Recent research builds on vast libraries of studies about the benefits of nature on well-being. Even shorter time periods and single experiences in natural settings hold value for mitigating negative moods and rumination.[2]

How to Use This Remedy

Train yourself to take notice, allow nature to engage your senses, and free your mind of painful thought shackles. Every day, purposefully spend half an hour in a natural spot. Almost anywhere will do. A trail, a park, a public garden, or an apartment terrace. The size or location matters less than your attentive presence. On a recent visit to a huge medical complex where I spent hours waiting during my husband's surgery, a bench under a tree provided respite from the slow ticking of anxious minutes. Cottony clouds in a sea blue sky, a few chirping birds, and the soft rustling of leaves in a gentle breeze that caressed my arms and face. In those moments, as numerous medical personnel and others waiting for loved ones in surgery passed by, I felt like a drop in the ocean of this great big world where people strive, struggle, and triumph every day.

A sense of awe can make you feel connected to, or insignificant in, a bigger purpose or system. Or you may simply marvel at the tiny worlds of nature in a trail of ants or the miracle of a moss patch. Wherever and however you find nature, take notice, get curious, and allow your senses to interact. Later, write about these brief experiences—how you felt, how your mind shifted, what you saw, smelled, or heard. Did you wonder about a flower, a bird, an insect, or a weather pattern? Take notes each day. Notice, appreciate, and engage. As John Muir says, "Every leaf seems to speak."[3] May your mind be free to hear.

"There will come soft rains and the smell of the ground,
And swallows circling with their shimmering sound."
—*Sara Teasdale* (1884–1933)

Remedy 17

Fresh Eyes

Initial Notes

When we first toured the older ranch-style home we moved to in early 2020, its high pine ceilings and windows galore dazzled us. We also loved its property strewn with majestic Heritage Oaks. Sure, there were some rough spots, but we overlooked those, and focused intently on the quiet, semi-rural neighborhood with an abundance of nimble wild turkeys and peaceful deer. Then we moved in and were faced with fixing all the problems.

The water heaters were rusted out. A broken, crumbling brick fountain marred the circular driveway. Spaces in the eaves harbored bats. The outside irrigation didn't work, the ancient toilets ran, and the old windows stuck and leaked—to name a few of the issues.

We began repairs at a time when the COVID-19 pandemic had shackled much of the world. Persuading workmen to come in person, assess needs, and tap elbows on a deal (the pandemic alternative to shaking hands) was close to impossible. Instead, they asked for texted explanations and pics. Then they gave non-binding bids. We did as much as we could by ourselves. On our wedding anniversary, I posted a picture of my husband and me, hefting a new window into an old one's space: "Forty years and still working together."

Four years after our move, relatives from another state visited for the first time. On a sunny spring morning, we walked around the perimeter of the house. Proud of the work we'd done, we also recounted the troubles we'd faced as we'd fixed this thing or solved that issue. As our relatives oohed and awed, I pointed out remaining flaws and future work. They saw only beauty.

Over the next several days, we relaxed into their visit, taking walks, showing them sights, or simply sitting in our gazebo, smelling the roses I had planted bare-root and nurtured over three seasons into their most stunning show yet. Near the end of their visit, I thanked them, saying, "I feel like I've seen this place with fresh eyes." Their visit had allowed me to see my home as I had that first day.

With heaps of personal obstacles rising as we'd done the work under the cloud of COVID, we'd traded a spirit of excitement and accomplishment for one of dread. That's just how it is when our minds race with imagined what-ifs. Rumination is the type of thinking that fails to shelter from the storm. The answer is to practice having "fresh eyes."

Why This Remedy Works

Most of us have heard the term "rose-colored glasses." I've talked to parents about how seeing their children activates reward centers in their brains.[1] Using this information about how the brain works to help them purposely remove their rose-colored glasses aids their objectivity toward their offspring. How and what we think about has the power to change our brains. "As the brain fires the brain wires" is a popular rhyme to explain neuroplasticity. Our brains can serve as superhighways of innovation, possibility, and good cheer. Or we can keep on ruminating, digging deeper ruts of negativity, worry, and despair. When we choose to look at ourselves and our situations with fresh eyes, we rewire our brains. In essence, by choosing new perspectives, we lay the inroads to more fruitful viewpoints and faster routes to solutions. The imaginal component of this exercise utilizes the anxiety-calming, optimism-inducing benefits of visualization.[2, 3]

How to Use This Remedy

Here, you'll imagine donning different reality glasses, which you will name, to provide a new view of rumination. Review your notes from prior remedies to help you determine what types of glasses might best help and then come up with a few names for different pairs. Then visualize what it's like to see through the glasses you choose. For example, if your thoughts often center on perceived personal failure, perhaps "Magic Mirror" glasses help you see yourself in a better light. A jumbled mess of disparate thoughts might require you to don "Clean-up Crew" spectacles and imagine sweeping out the mess. Perhaps you'll prescribe "Optimistic Bifocals" that help you identify pessimistic thoughts and trade them for an optimistic view. If you're angry, don some "Love Lenses" and find something of benefit in the subject of your rumination. Even a lesson you wouldn't necessarily choose can help you in the future.

On the lines that follow, borrow my examples or come up with several of your own. Choose ones that fit your ruminative patterns and content based on your review. Add a line after each about what function they will serve.

Then, when faced with negative cognition, close your eyes and visualize yourself donning the glasses that best fit. Imagine seeing your thoughts and their content through the chosen glasses. Visualize action based on your chosen lens prescription. Wearing the glasses, what do you do differently? How does the view change?

As you use different glasses during different ruminative episodes, write about your experiences with this technique. Adjust your prescription as needed.

Additional Tips and Techniques

Negative thought loops are circular in nature. Mentally, rumination is like looking at the same scene over and over, often with increasing distress. One way to break the cycle is to move to a new view. Go to the window, walk out the door, or change the angle at which you normally look at your living room, or some other view. Look more closely at something such as your pet's paws, the patterned leaves on a potted plant, or a tree's bark. A literal shift in your view brings fresh eyes that disrupt the interior refrain.

_____

_____

_____

_____

_____

_____

_____

_____

Remedy 18

What Would Batman, Jesus, or the Dalai Lama Do?

Initial Notes

Years ago, before a writing conference, I contemplated the schedule with trepidation. The prospect of approaching editors and agents at a mixer event distressed me. I'm an introvert, so my mouth went dry at the thought of introducing myself. And if I got that far, what would I say about my book? Once at the conference, I hung back, my mind racing with imagined disasters like me standing tongue-tied or knocking over a VIP's drink, as fellow writers mingled and schmoozed like pros.

Determined not to let the opportunity pass unseized, I asked a friend who flitted from agent to editor to agent and then back to our table how she managed. *Her answer*? "Just pretend you're someone else." So, as she headed off to mix and mingle, I conjured up a more confident vision of myself. What would Sheri 2.0 say? How would she stand, speak, and shake someone's hand? The idea worked. With this self-assured, already successful alter ego in mind, I devised pitch lines and set about the process of networking with surprising ease.

This phenomenon is known as the "Batman effect," from research on self-distancing done with children.[1] The kids who took on the persona of a character such as Dora the Explorer or Batman enjoyed more confidence and a 23 percent increase in focus on a study task over those who thought of themselves in the first person. Even kids who referred to themselves using their own names (third-person) versus thinking of themselves as "I," performed 13 percent better. If I'd have known this all those years ago, I might have switched out my Sheri 2.0 persona for one channeling Stephen King or Agatha Christie.

What does any of this have to do with ruminating? Well, having experienced firsthand the benefits of an alter ego, I've used a similar technique for negative self-talk and a racing mind. Instead of lying in the darkness, thoughts twisting and turning on some stressor, I assign a disruptor in the form of an alter ego with the same dilemma or concern. What would the Golden Girls' innocent Rose Nyland say or do? How about wise Dorothy, sarcastic Sophia, or sultry Blanche Deveraux? Imagining a famous person—whether funny, competent, or with superpowers—delivering a mic-drop one-liner, flouncing out of a room with chin held high, or making quick work of a problem can dissolve tension.

Why This Remedy Works

When you purposely transfer cerebral energy from emotional distress to creativity, you provide the padding of emotional distance we've talked about previously. Imagining yourself as a chosen alter ego activates different brain regions and frees up brainpower to think from a novel perspective. Beyond the boundaries of your personal muck, solutions may drop into your mind like gifts. An alter ego's imagined comeback might shift you from crying out to laughing out loud. You may feel stronger, more competent, and banish your fears. A new perspective can make your future look brighter. Or, as Captain Kirk might think, you'll go more boldly than you've ever gone before.

How to Use This Remedy

This week, come up with a few alter egos. You can choose fictional characters, superheroes, or real figures whether celebrity, historical, or from your personal life. The trick is to know them well. Fictional characters can already exist or be ones you dream up and endow with certain qualities and strengths. Pop star Beyonce came up with "Sasha Fierce" to help her perform with more confidence. Singer Adele took on her alter ego "Sasha Carter." You can name yours whatever you want.

On the lines below, jot down a few alter egos you're drawn to.

_____

_____

_____

Now, for your choices, write down their qualities you believe will be helpful. In each alter ego's voice, add one-liners, jokes, or affirmations. For existing characters, reflect upon the clothing they wear, the way they talk, their worldview, and more. Then, as needed, ask yourself, "What would XX do?" Imagine what they'd tell themselves (and others), how they'd carry themselves, and how they'd feel.

Additional Tips and Techniques

For AI users—If you've chosen a well-known person or character for your alter ego, prompt AI to generate ideas. What might Eleanor Roosevelt say about criticism? How would President XX handle worry? What are some Ghandi quotes about letting go?

You can choose whoever you think would be helpful—no limits. Try a TV character, the old talking horse Mr. Ed, or an archetypal figure from mythology or a fictional work. Conjure your alter ego to guide you to peace.

RUMINATION REMEDIES

Remedy 19

Thrival, It's in Your Genes

Initial Notes

My Native American ancestors were driven from their homelands and relocated on the "Trail of Tears." They suffered hardships. Some died but many survived *and endured*. I'm living proof of their survival, or as I like to call it their "thrival" spirit. No matter who *you* are, ancestors in your history also prevailed. If they hadn't, you wouldn't exist. Moving beyond troubles is in your genes. *You're living proof.*

In the above paragraph, I switched from my singular experience as a person of specific descent to a more global human experience. It's another example of the distancing you practiced by using your name in Remedy 5, *Who's That You're Talking To?*

In your self-talk, after using your own name to grab attention and generate emotional distance, it's natural to switch to a universal you. Now might be a good time to look back at the examples from that section to see the progression. Or here's a new (and real) example: "Sheri, stop editing as you write. It only slows you down."

This week's remedy has two distinct tasks:

1. To identify with and draw strength from your kin.

2. To inspire positive self-talk using the universal you (from what you know or learn about their hardships and endurance).

Why This Remedy Works

A sense of belonging increases the inspiration we draw from others' examples.[1] Using the universal you in our self-talk is a form of distancing, which gives us an outsider's perspective to our problems.[2, 3] Also, the universal you provides two levels of distancing because it mimics the second-person encouragement we receive from others. It's familiar from the earliest ages of learning when we internalized "you" to regulate our behavior.[4]

How to Use This Remedy

Task #1—What do you know of your family history? Find a big-picture theme such as my Trail of Tears ancestry or focus on individuals from your family tree. Consider their survival (and thrival). What did they endure? Overcome? Shrug off and thrive despite? No need to understand every detail. If you know your ancestors are from Scandinavia, for example, a quick internet search for history can reveal some struggles as well as wins. Ditto for just about any other ancestral origins.

If you don't know your specific family history, no matter. You're a member of humanity and can choose from present-day and historical figures you admire. Draw strength from their resilience. Or, look to more generalized historical themes such as the Great Depression, the American pioneers' quest for a better life out West, or the pilgrims seeking religious freedom. Choose what works for you. Draw inspiration from people's courage in the face of obstacles. They navigated difficulties, survived, and procreated. Their will to thrive is working in humanity, thus in you.

Generational trauma is real and can provide insight into your unique struggles, but the fact remains, someone endured and moved forward. So can *you*.

Jot a few notes about your chosen ancestors, individual figures, or generalized population of an era, what they endured, and how they triumphed. Then, write down specific words that summarize their strengths. Also, consider what it is about their fortitude and resourcefulness that inspires you? How can you apply that in your own life? My ancestors learned to adapt, and that's a quality I borrow from and use in my own thrival every day. How about yours and you?

_____

_____

_____

_____

Additional Tips and Techniques

Choose to focus on your ancestors' music or another form of rejoicing. Research their music, dance, or art. How did their suffering figure into their creativity? How can you draw strength from the hope, discipline, or resilience you see or hear in their art? How can you identify with their music, dance, or other creative expressions? As an example, my tribe (The Muscogee Creek Nation) adapted to European influence in elaborate and colorful apparel they styled in unique ways. I love colorful clothing and sometimes choose apparel as costumes to fit specific roles or set the mood. One tunic with an elaborate design has served as my "armor" for difficult situations. Where does your creative expression or appreciation fit in with that of your ancestors?

Task # 2—Spend a few minutes forming universal "you" statements about your own struggles that borrow from your ancestors' strengths and use the words you identified in Task #1. For example, I might tell myself, *"You can adapt."*

During ruminative episodes or as you notice your inner dialogue dipping into defeatist "I" statements, make a conscious effort to interrupt the pattern and draw from your reflections to insert encouraging words. You *belong* in a long line of human beings who endured and thrived. Crafting powerful statements that remind you of your built-in strength makes shifting toward self-encouragement and grit second nature.

Remedy 20

A Routine to Remember

Initial Notes

At a stunt cycle event at the local fair, the announcer yammered on as one rider revved his motorcycle into the arena and stopped at the curve of the long, oval track. In quick succession, he kissed the cross on his neck chain, lifted his face and hands skyward, mouthed a prayer, made the sign of the cross on his chest, and bowed his head. I watched with interest as he stopped at each of the remaining three curves of the track and repeated the ritual. When his amazing run was over, he stopped near the exit gate, got off his bike, and did a similar routine on bended knee.

That was the first time I'd seen such an easily spotted performance ritual, but they are by no means uncommon. The use of rituals, which calms anxiety, quells negative thinking, and improves performance,[1] is rampant among athletes, speakers, singers, and the like. After all, the show must go on.

You may not be performing in a stunt cycle event but, at times, the stakes of life can feel as high. To live well and be happy, you must show up and go on. When mental anguish and worry deplete your energy, it's tough to show up for anything. Rituals can help.

Before your imagination is shaped by the word "ritual," let me assure you that rituals are not always religious, formal, or on public display. In fact, you may be engaging in one regularly—without even realizing. A simple ritual can provide comfort, confidence, and security, as well as aid feelings of readiness and head off a bout of mental torment.

Throughout the world's cultures and history, rituals are associated with transitional times of anxiety and stress such as births, weddings, and deaths. The same sorts of times that may be giving *you* anxiety and amping up worrisome, ruminative thoughts. But some researchers have come to understand that ritualized behavior stems from anxiety and occurs more naturally, such as the way anxious public speakers may spontaneously repeat hand gestures.[2]

Even so, most agree that, to define a ritual, three elements must be present:

1. A fixed sequence. (An ordered, structured repetition.)

2. No instrumental value. (The behavior doesn't connect in a practical way to a task at hand. For example, the stunt cyclist's ritual didn't relate to his riding.)

3. Symbolic meaning. (Often spiritual or connected to culture but can be personal in meaning.)

Though this has been the typical view, a ritual need not always be so formal. Each evening, I pull out a special mug for tea. In it, one bag of organic chamomile is coupled with another from my chosen variety of anti-stress, anti-anxiety, or calming blends kept on hand. Symbolically, it's my way of switching gears from a busy day, exposed to many people with their unique stories and their energy, toward a quieter evening. Ritualized by the routine and the comfort this activity brings me, *a* cup of tea has become *my* cup of tea, which is how Bradd Shore, a cultural anthropologist and author of *The Hidden Power of Rituals*, describes the natural process of a behavior's ritualization.[3]

Why This Remedy Works

Research into anxious thinking posits several reasons why rituals are effective help. One is that ritualized behavior creates order, bringing a sense of realized expectation to the uncertain.[4,5] Additionally, performing a ritual distracts focus from intrusive thoughts and takes up working memory, busying the brain out of rumination.[6,7] The meaning and symbolism of a ritual transcend the human experience of self, which provides a buffer to fear of threat or uncertainty.[8,9] The stunt cyclist's pre- and post-ride prayers come to mind. Whether religious or not, what you believe about the power of a ritual matters, which is why so many engage in routines that seem meaningless to outsiders, such as eating a "lucky" pre-game meal.[10] If you believe a specific ritual helps you prior to an important work meeting, a high-conflict family conversation, or before sleep, you're surely helped.

How to Use This Remedy

First, consider any rituals you already incorporate (now or in the past) into your life. Perhaps "your" cup of tea has become ritualized like mine or you understand from the performing arts or participation in sports how anxiety-busting ritualized behavior can be. On the lines here, identify any past or present ritualized behavior you've engaged in. Write about your associated beliefs and their origin, as well as how the rituals helped.

Don't overlook the simplest rituals. For example, a morning bowl of oatmeal becomes a ritual if it takes on meaning and importance, i.e., you consider it necessary for energy and intestinal regularity, and you worry that when you don't eat it you won't feel good. Your beliefs about the power of a ritual become like links in a chain, strengthening your commitment to the ritual. For instance, you make sure "your" oatmeal is always on hand, even taking it along when you travel so you can be sure to continue the routine.

The same is true of "my" nightly tea, ritualized by general time of night, the mug used, and the mental debriefing from my day that has long become habit and clears my mind for the evening. I often fix another just before bed and, if I awaken in the night, a sip or two reminds my mind to empty of worrisome thoughts and my physical body to relax. My tea is symbolic for shifting into peace and rest.

Remember, even if your ritual seemed silly, if you believed it worked, it probably did as the research indicates.

If you've identified a few rituals that have worked for you, your task is to apply them now. Feel free to borrow from, combine, or alter for current situations and ongoing rumination loops. Nightly prayer for children of any age is a helpful go-to for many parents. As are prayers for the wisdom and strength to let go and let God, or generally let problems go. Maybe you have ritualized the wearing of a particular clothing item or the order in which you perform a particular task.

Whether you have rituals to turn to or are coming to this fresh, consider what could help you now. To shift your focus from mental anguish, reciting a particular poem, or reading from a book by a specific author might serve to distract and provide meaning. John Muir's nature essays could be a viable option, for example, connecting you to seasonal rhythms of nature and something bigger than yourself. One woman in her 70s, whose family has abandoned her, told me of her ritual of shuffling through a collection of uplifting memes she has curated off the internet. Looking at the meme set with their familiar photos and sayings calms her restless mind and helps her feel settled for sleep each evening. That's a "ritual."

What ritual could *you* do? Use the lines below to brainstorm ideas. Then test them out and write about your experiences.

___

___

___

___

___

___

___

___

"There is a magic in the morning when the day is new
and we shape it with our quiet customs."
—*Kate Douglas Wiggin* (1856–1923)

Remedy 21

The Mother's Touch

Initial Notes

As a kid making mud pies and running barefoot all summer, I didn't know that my tactile connection to Mother Earth was nurturing me. Sound sleep, boundless energy, and the ability to shift from distress to a happy-go-lucky outlook often came easily. Maybe some of that is natural to all children, but as an older adult, I learned about the benefits of plugging into the Earth's energy via direct contact. Research makes the benefits of a practice known as "earthing" clear. Connecting to Earth energy is what this remedy is about.

Why This Remedy Works

The Earth's surface is charged with an ever-replenishing supply of mobile electrons and, except in very dry areas like deserts, is electrically conductive. Numerous studies demonstrate that "grounding" our bodies to the Earth, similar to the way electrical outlets in our homes are grounded for safety, is beneficial. With studies examining everything from the effects on wound healing to improved vagal tone, there's a growing body of scientific research about the benefits of earthing. Noted are reductions in inflammation, pain, and the stress hormone cortisol. Mental clarity and nervous system calming are enhanced.

No wonder there's increased interest in this practice that was natural and instinctive to the people of ancient cultures. They lived more earthy lives, wearing shoes made of animal skin and sleeping on the ground. Even philosophers including Aristotle and Plato recommended contact with the Earth for its balancing energy. The Greeks incorporated the need for such direct contact into their architecture. With earthing, people today report feeling more relaxed and emotionally steady, getting better sleep, and enjoying an improved mood.[1,2,3,4,5] That's all good news for ruminators.

How to Use This Remedy

As the elements allow, let your skin touch the Earth or its natural waterways.

The easiest way to get started is to walk or stand barefoot on grass, sand, soil, or rock. Especially if your feet are sensitive, begin with exposure in small time intervals. You could slip off your shoes for a few minutes while watering plants with a hose, for example. Tell yourself you're getting grounded as you plug into Mother Earth.

Getting your hands on the ground or in the dirt is another option. You can do this while gardening or just sitting with your hands resting on the soil. In a pleasant setting where the grass isn't treated with potentially harmful chemicals, you could sit back while propping your weight on your forearms. Expose your legs, too, if it feels right to you. Gardeners sometimes weed their growing beds while on their hands and knees. They're earthing.

Don't overlook water for its grounding properties. Swimming in the ocean or a lake is more than invigorating. These water bodies are also grounding. Wade in a shallow creek or simply stand in wet sand or wet grass for benefits. While I've never been hooked up to measuring devices for proof, some of my most earth-charged moments have been when dipping my feet into rushing river water or a cool, clear lake.

Living trees with their roots in the earth are grounded entities. Tree hugging has real benefits, so go do that if the mood strikes. Lean against a tree or run your fingertips along its rough, scaled, or smooth bark. For purposes of earthing, which is also sometimes called "grounding," you can't bark up the wrong tree. Um, unless you're allergic, or the tree is ant- or otherwise infested. Any vegetation that's rooted is grounded, so pulling weeds also counts as earthing.

Don't neglect multi-level earthing. Consider a brisk ocean swim that gets your skin tingling and then lying back without a towel in the sun-warmed sand. Next, get your hands into the sand and build a castle. Or dig a hole and dip your feet when the tide fills it.

How else might you get in touch with this mother of all remedies that's free? Start by listing your options. Then make earthing a part of every possible day. As you earth, be mindful of the present moment and any sights, sounds, and scents. Notice the texture of the grass, the warmth of the soil, and so on. How do you feel both inside and out? With a routine practice of earthing, do you sleep better? Are you more relaxed? Did you find yourself smiling during the sessions? How about later? Write about the experiences. If fun and awe become a part of your practice, all the better.

 **Additional Tips and Techniques**

If natural grounding isn't an option because of weather or lack of access to nature, you can get in touch with the earth's grounding properties indoors with products specifically made for this purpose. Plug-in grounding mats allow you to tap into the Earth's natural charge. You can place a mat under your feet at your desk, and companies also offer sheets, pillowcases, and mats for the bed. There are many suppliers. You'll want to research price and reliability as you would with any product. I've used a variety of these products and have found them useful.

Remedy 22

Learning Curve, Building Bridges

Initial Notes

In the first and second *Learning Curve* sections, you learned about the *why* behind your energetic fire for positive change (your "Wi-Fi") as well as how and why review is important for learning and changing behavior. Those ideas are embedded here as well, but this time, we focus on thinking about thinking, that is "metacognition," and using it in ways that help.

Why Structured Metacognition Helps

You may have caught yourself saying something like, "I can't stop thinking about this," or "My mind just won't let this go." Awareness is the first step to breaking the automatic loops of ruminative thinking and preparing you to make a shift.[1] But awareness alone doesn't fix anything. In fact, those statements are infused with a sense of helpless desperation that makes the problem feel insurmountable. The workbook's structure, along with your efforts and monitored success, helps you bridge the gap between your overthinking and your control. Seeing this progress reinforces your motivation, fueling your growth.[2]

As you've gone through the workbook so far, trying techniques and measuring the effects, you've checked your understanding, recognized what you've mastered, and identified where you need to improve. You've also noted what worked for you and what didn't. Such awareness is a form of "self-regulated learning," which has prepared you to adapt the strategies to best fit you.[3] Take a moment to consider this on the lines just below. Write about what you've mastered and areas where you've identified your need to improve. This will help you transfer what you've learned to new situations.[4, 5] Taking charge of your thinking via structured metacognition and awareness can reduce the anxiety that's so often associated with rumination. You'll increase confidence that you *can* be in control. Don't forget to tell yourself that.[6]

___

Measure Your Progress

Of the skills covered in Remedies 13–21, which have you experimented with? Below, you'll find each of the techniques listed along with an explanatory line intended to jog your memory. To the left, check off or draw a star next to each of the techniques you've experimented with.

Review your notes and reflect upon each experience. Run through the steps again if that feels necessary. Then, using a scale of 0-10 where ten means super helpful and zero means not helpful all, write the number that best represents your experience with each technique (on the line to the right).

_____ **13: Making Tomorrow Real** *(Get in touch with your future self.)* _____

_____ **14: N-E-W** *(Create an acronym and use it to help.)* _____

_____ **15: You're Here Now, and Safe** *(Grounding Methods.)* _____

_____ **16: Awestruck** *(The power of nature.)* _____

_____ **17: Fresh Eyes** *(Seeing things from a new perspective)* _____

_____ **18: What Would Batman, Jesus, or the Dalai Lama Do?** *(Using alter egos.)* _____

_____ **19: Thrival, It's in Your Genes** *(Leaning on the resilience of ancestors.)* _____

_____ **20: A Routine to Remember** *(Behavioral rituals for comfort and confidence.)* _____

_____ **21: The Mother's Touch** *("Earthing" techniques for well-being.)* _____

Catch Up or Toss

Did you skip any of the techniques entirely? Or, do you feel you didn't give some techniques adequate effort? Now is the time to go back and experiment with ones you believe warrant additional exploration. You might also consider any *Additional Tips and Techniques* boxes you neglected. Rate or re-rate techniques as needed.

What Didn't Help?

Review any exercises you considered *un*helpful and reflect upon what didn't resonate and why. After considering anything you deemed *un*helpful, do further journaling, seek a compassionate ear, or simply bid farewell to any tools so far that don't resonate. Pointing out what didn't work for you is a valuable way to dispel negative energy and let it go. Use the lines here for that purpose.

_____

_____

_____

Favorites So Far

Using your ratings of Remedies 13–21, note the tools you found most helpful. Consider why these worked. What did you like about them? How easy were they to implement and remember?

Reflecting here will provide insight into the best times for you to experiment as well as how to make the techniques more your own. After journaling about your favorites, use the last block of lines in this *Learning Curve* to record the titles of your favorites among Remedies 13–21.

_____

_____

_____

_____

My Go-Tos

Remedy 23

Pour It Out

Initial Notes

For me, the act of journaling was foiled when, at age 16, I recounted a double date I went on with a good school friend and two boys. Always the creative writer, I embellished the *actual* events to include my teenage fantasy—all in good fun until my friend called the next afternoon to tell me that her mother had received a phone call from mine. Apparently, my mom read my racy rendition as real. My friend said her mother laughed at my flowery prose, disbelieving those awkward boys had the smooth-operator prowess I'd described. *She* recognized a teen girl's imaginings as anything but real, even if my own mom didn't. A few hours later, I was called to the carpet. My mother wouldn't listen when I recounted the limp innocence of the actual date with dull boys who chewed sugary bubble gum, arm wrestled over the Arby's table, and talked about nothing but cars.

After that, I didn't keep a journal again for decades. That's too bad because journaling is known for its many benefits including mental clarity, improved focus, better problem-solving, and an elevated mood.

Why This Remedy Works

Journaling about emotionally rich material including trauma is a form of "expressive writing," which has been studied for decades as an effective way to process emotions, view real or even imagined events from new perspectives, increase self-awareness, gain clarity, and relieve stress. The benefits are not only psychological but physical.[1] It's helpful to dump thoughts and feelings onto paper (or a computer screen), which shifts them from a tangled, balled-up knot in the mind and strings it all out where it can be (and feel) more organized, and be brought to clarity. Journaling about your ruminations, worries, negative thoughts, and feelings helps. That's why we've used it so much in the workbook. This week, we're formalizing the process as a separate and beneficial exercise.

How to Use This Remedy

Choose one or both of the following methods.

METHOD ONE: *Routine*

One way to utilize journaling is as a preemptive measure. Meaning that you journal as a regular practice. This is the way the well-known "gratitude" journaling is used, which is a practice of reflecting upon one's day and recording any moments, events, people, or conditions worthy of thanks. For the purpose of the work you're doing here, the focus will be on what troubles you, which allows for some thought dumping but is structured for beneficial metacognitive processing. This clears the mind before a ruminative episode takes hold as well as sparks deeper insights toward gaining peace.

If you choose to do this exercise in this way, your practice of written expression requires a private space, a journal (notebook or computer), and one or more of the suggested prompts. Therapeutic "expressive writing" practices usually ask participants to play soft background music and discuss their writing with someone else. I'll leave those options up to you. Let yourself be free of worries over grammar or spelling—you're not going for public consumption or grades. If you did decide to share your writings in a blog, book, or with a friend or therapist, you could edit as needed, including choosing sections deemed most significant.

Over time, particularly if you find yourself writing about the same worries or regrets, try shaping the writing with more intention. Reflect upon your realizations and insights. As you journal, use language that supports those insights, i.e., words such as *realize*, *because*, *understand*, *conclude*, etc. Routine journaling can be transformational in how you think about yourself in relation to the world, your life, and other people. The prompts here are intended to get you there quickly.

To use the Routine method, commit to a time each day, or at least three days per week, when you will journal. Fifteen to twenty minutes is adequate. Schedule your sessions wisely. If you're new to journaling, be aware that writing about troubles can be unsettling at first. Allow time afterward to shift gears and decompress before returning to your day. Plan a short walk outdoors, as an example (and use the ideas from Remedy 26). Or engage in a small ritual such as drinking a glass of water or chewing gum to refocus.

Follows are some prompts to apply to whatever overthinking you choose to journal about. I've used the universal "you" to build in beneficial distancing. Choose one or more prompts per journaling session.

1. What is the actual "fear" that goes along with or is behind this thinking?
2. Is this worry/issue within your power to fix?
3. What parts of this issue/problem/worry are within your responsibility or power to control?
4. Have you experienced something previously that relates to or is like this worry or issue? How? And what can you learn from that experience that's applicable to this one?
5. How does this thinking affect your body? How does your body feel? Are your shoulders tight? Is your jaw clenched? Is your tummy upset? Etc.
6. What are several words that name the feelings that go with this?
7. If you were asked to make a bulleted list that represents the content of your thinking about this issue or event, what would the listed bullets be?
8. What questions could you ask yourself that would help you adopt a new perspective?
9. What has changed about how you think about this? What needs to change?
10. What has changed about who you are in relation to this?
11. What are some positive results?
12. In light of the positive results (number 11), what is stopping you from further developing those?
13. What is the worst-case scenario? Does it make sense? (See Remedy 35.)
14. If you were a funny person, what about yourself would make you laugh in this scenario?
15. If you were Jesus Christ, the Dalai Lama, Buddha (or another wise figure you choose), what insights would you impart to yourself?
16. If a loved one came to you with this, what would you tell them? How would you sound as you said the words? What might you do? (Can you apply these now, to yourself?)
17. Are you being too hard on yourself? How? Have you been too hard on yourself in the past?
18. How can you give yourself grace?
19. How many hours have you spent thinking about this (or in this manner)? Has it helped? How much more time makes sense to spend on this (or in this way)?
20. If you were truly wise, you would ... *fill in the blank.*

METHOD TWO: *In the Moment*

This second method is an emergency measure. You find yourself unable to quiet your mind and you reach for your journal. Go to a quiet space and pour out your emotions and distress. Freely express or use the above prompts. You can use the lines I've provided with this exercise to start, but you'll need your own supplies over time (journal, notebook, computer).

Additional Tips and Techniques

If you've been following along sequentially, you won't be surprised that I find a cup of soothing tea accompanies journaling well. What would you find comforting as you journal? Write down your ideas here and try them as you utilize this exercise.

_____

_____

_____

_____

_____

_____

_____

_____

"My diary is a shelter — a place where my soul may breathe."
—*Christina Rossetti* (1830–1894)

> "I make the page my confidante."
> —*Sara Teasdale* (1884–1933)

Remedy 24

Say It to the Dolls

Initial Notes

One year on a trip to a writing conference, I found myself worrying about my children back at home with their dad. Would they get off to school okay? Would they make it back home safely? My mind twisted on imagined scenarios. I barely slept. That's when I came across "worry dolls" in a hotel gift shop and was fascinated by their story.

The tiny dolls made of bits of wood and scraps of colorful fabric derive from ancient Mayan culture, proving that a troubled mind isn't anything new. It was believed you could whisper your worries to the dolls, tuck them under your pillow, and drift off to blissful sleep knowing the dolls were working on your problems overnight.

Although I didn't believe the dolls were imbued with magic, the idea of giving over my worries meant getting the thoughts out of my head. Besides, the tiny stick figures dressed in bright garb were adorably cute. I purchased a set of inch-long figures that came with a drawstring bag and, that night, held each up, purposefully calling my worries to mind. I didn't whisper as instructed but thought of my worries as I looked into their dot-of-paint eyes and then tucked each doll back into the bag. Like magic, I slept well that night and was ready for a long day of conference events in the morning.

That experience, and the reasons behind its effectiveness, form the basis for this week's exercise. Don't worry. I won't ask you to play with dolls (unless you want to).

Why This Remedy Works

As with journaling (Remedy 23), just dumping the thoughts out of your head helps. Also, as is true with a ritual (Remedy 20), *believing* something will work is effective. You don't have to believe the dolls will work on your problems as the lore goes, but do invest in the very real prospect that unloading your worries works. You could just as easily hold another figurine or some other item that fulfills the listener role. And, as my experience demonstrates, you don't have to speak to them out loud either. For that matter, why limit this to bedtime?

How to Use This Remedy

If a set of worry dolls appeals to you, obtain some and use them. They're easily found online. Otherwise, find a substitute. Pet a furry friend and confide your troubles, for example. Then, go on to sleep or proceed with your day.

Additional Tips and Techniques

Here are two alternatives that draw on the idea of worry dolls:

- Get a pocket-sized notebook and write out your problems/worries in concise language (think bullets). Then fold the pages and put them in a special box, bag, or envelope. Put them somewhere safe (maybe under your pillow).

- Close your eyes and hold a trusted individual, real or created, in your mind's eye. Imagine telling your problems to that wise and caring person. Many people talk to departed loved ones in this way and re-experience, through the power of memory and imagination, the love and care they once felt.

What was it like to do this exercise? Write about how you participated as well as your feelings and the results.

_____

_____

_____

Remedy 25

Normalize

Initial Notes

Some of the most traumatizing incidents of my life have been accompanied by loneliness. When my mother committed suicide, I confided in people whose responses made it clear they couldn't relate. Their reactions made me feel more alone. I was less keen to share my feelings again. Even a therapist was more interested in speculating about my mother's childhood than in helping me heal. In my isolation, I sometimes blamed myself. I should have seen it coming, called Mom earlier that day, said this or done that last week, last month, or even last year. I kept busy but in the quiet moments, ruminating ruled.

Then I got my first computer and connected to the internet. As it turns out, I wasn't as alone as I thought. Neither are you, no matter your troubles. The 1993 R.E.M. song says it best, "Everybody Hurts." In today's world where virtual connection is at our fingertips, we can search for and find fellow sufferers, information, and advice for just about any hurt, stress, or worry. That's the crux of this week's exercise.

As an aside, you have a copy of this workbook to help manage your thoughts. *You're not the only one.* You're in a vast tribe of people suffering in their rumination, negative self-talk, or worry. The style or content of the thoughts may be specific to you, but even that is likely less rare than you might think.

Why This Remedy Works

Finding out we aren't the only ones helps us to realize we aren't stupid, strange, or silly. We're human, enduring the human experience. This normalizes our situation and our response to it. We find that our feelings are more common than we thought and, if others have succeeded at working through similar situations, we can too. Also, seeing other people with similar worries or regrets can provide the benefit of distance. It's easier to solve someone else's concerns because we're not so mired in the problems or invested in the outcomes. The distance makes us more open to solutions. We can borrow for our own lives the critical thinking and advice that come to mind for another.

How to Use This Remedy

Reflect upon the content of your most frequent troublesome thoughts. Do you ruminate over what was or what you miss(ed)? Or, are you worrying over what will be? Who or what is most often prominent in your thinking? Review your notes from Remedies 1 and 2 to identify the specifics. Consider how much your thoughts have changed since you began the workbook. Then drill down to a few short representative phrases for now.

Not long ago, I mentioned something to a friend about his "inner critic." He pondered the term and said he had never thought of his "negative self-talk" like that, yet he's an old pro at what he puts another way: "Beating myself up." An internet search for peer support for any of those terms finds people like him, struggling with a mean inner voice.

A sense of belonging, whether you participate in groups or simply read about people who hold similar feelings/thoughts, is edifying and has a calming effect. Your brain can shift out of the emotional chaos that comes with a stirred up central nervous system and into its more logical thinking mode of the prefrontal cortex. That's where possible solutions can be evaluated, implemented, and reviewed for effectiveness.

Use some of the lines provided to write out the triggers, content, and style of your most frequent troublesome thoughts. For a few minutes, remember to breathe naturally as you dwell on these thoughts. You might also hug yourself, place your hand on your heart, or otherwise comfort yourself somatically. Then devise a key phrase and do a search online. If you don't find much with one phrase, tweak it and search again. Try using quotation marks around phrases. Read beyond the first few listed results (or even pages of results). With a bit of digging, you will find that you're not alone. You will normalize your thinking.

Spend some time this week searching and reading through results. *You're not alone.* Take notes about engaging in this technique. Use the lines included here to write about the experience. What surprised you about your findings? What didn't? How does normalizing your difficult thinking patterns help? Does a logical next step come to mind? (For example, many people subscribe to my free newsletter. Or they join my membership for parents of estranged adult children where they can share concerns, get from-the-trenches support and advice, and learn how to let go and move forward despite the loss.)

Additional Tips and Techniques

- If you wake up in the night, sit in the dark after dinner, or languish in bed in the morning with worries or what-ifs, lean on the helpful information and support you've found. Get up, move to a new space, and seek out bookmarked websites or books that provide you with proof you're not alone. Journal about new (and old) readings.

- If you already belong to an online support/member site where you find comfort, log on. Put your thoughts down in the group where you can generate caring responses of support.

Remedy 26

Solvitur Ambulando

Initial Notes

Putting one foot in front of the other for a mile or more each morning has always been as good for my head as it is my heart. I'm not the only one. The Latin phrase, *solvitur ambulando* or "it is solved by walking," is an idea that dates to antiquity. Much of Aristotle's teaching took place on foot. Great thinkers across time, including Charles Darwin, Ralph Waldo Emerson, Henry David Thoreau, and Thomas Jefferson, knew their feet held a key to cognitive processing.[1]

That movement and thinking are intertwined is reflected in common language. One instantly understands taking a walk to clear your head. Terms such as "moving forward" or "moving on" imply leaving the undesirable or unsolvable behind and "advancing" toward new goals. These all indicate forward momentum and are emotionally much better than being "stuck" or "at a standstill."[1]

This remedy will have you stepping away from negative thinking loops that leave you stalled, going nowhere or in circles. Leave all that behind. It's time to step out, move beyond the problem, and finally get somewhere with peace.

Why This Remedy Works

Physical movement serves as a cognitive disruptor, so moving your body takes you out of your head. Additionally, walking aids creative thinking.[2] Movement breaks those negative thinking loops that play on a dizzying autopilot. Finally, a habit of walking can change your body's chemistry, making you more biologically resilient. A sedentary lifestyle contributes to higher cortisol spikes that remain higher longer than when engaged in a regular walking routine. Lower stress hormones allow for more peace—in our bodies and in our minds.[3]

How to Use This Remedy

When you notice yourself feeling anxious and your mind is spinning, looping, or fixating on unhelpful thoughts, tell yourself you're leaving that behind—and then do. Literally, get up, step out, and walk away from the thoughts. Circle the block, head over the mountain, or simply stroll to the garage and back. Intentionally shift your thoughts. Conceptual metaphors can result in concrete realities. We benefit from language that represents momentum and ease.[4, 5]

As you physically get up to disrupt, and then literally move away from your negative thoughts, talk to yourself in ways that represent where you want to be and how you want to feel. Use the universal you to reap the related benefits (discussed earlier in the book). Have fun with this and get as creative as you'd like. Tell yourself things like:

- You're really moving along.
- You're stepping effortlessly forward.
- You're gliding along on a breeze.
- You're really getting somewhere now.
- You're stepping up/out.
- You're on your way.
- All the elements are supporting you.

You can also use this exercise preemptively. By walking routinely, you shape your body's response to stress so that it is less reactive.[3] On any given morning, you might see me walking up and down the hills near my home. I'll be telling myself, "Sheri, you are hopping to it. Way to move. The Earth is supporting you. The birds are singing praise." Yeah, it can all feel silly—and a little silliness is good for the soul.

As you experiment with this exercise, keep track of your activity and experiences. How does *walking away* from your troubles work for you? How does *stepping to a new beat* make you feel? Do you recognize the connection between your feet, your forward momentum, and your thoughts? Record your ideas and progress on the lines.

Additional Tips and Techniques

If your circumstances permit, consider creating a "moon garden" where you can safely cut a forward path. The idea of a moon garden filled with silvery leaves and white blooms that will glow in lunar light has been around at least since the early 1800s. The Chicago Botanical Garden website reports on an 1833 moon garden designed by Benjamine Poore in Massachusetts and shares an 1888 seed catalog illustration showing a woman strolling in a garden lit by the moon. Choose blooming plants that glow in the moonlight and release a pleasing evening scent. I've added whimsical solar lights to make my nighttime strolls safer. With a path through a special garden meant for nighttime enjoyment, disrupt your negative thinking and drink in the moonlight poet Jamie Sabines calls a "tonic."

Even inside the home, nightlights that come on automatically can form a path up the hall, around the coffee table, to the window, and back. Patios and decks can also make good moon garden paths.

"When my legs move, my thoughts flow."
—*Henry David Thoreau* (1817–1862)

Remedy 27

Touchstones and Talismans

Initial Notes

My husband swung the sledgehammer, and the old shower tile splintered, sending up a cloud of dust. I covered my nose, immediately having second thoughts about remodeling our bathroom. The mess, the noise, the unexpected problems that always arise.... What were we getting ourselves into?

After dinner that night, I switched on the bathroom light and was startled by movement in the sink. A cricket. The Jerusalem or "baby faced" cricket had apparently come up through the drain. I cringed, my mind seizing upon stored imagery from the "invasion" movies of my childhood. One look at the hapless fellow attempting to climb the steep sides of the porcelain sink, and I imagined clusters of them pushing up through the drain, antennae wriggling, the scraping sound of their tiny feet slipping backward magnified.

But there's only one. One of those odd, big-headed ones, but still, a harmless cricket.

Inwardly cursing the broken drain plug, I scooped the squirmy creature into a cup and covered the top with a paper towel. Once he was safely deposited outdoors, I told my youngest adult daughter about the incident. "Kinda gross," I said, another B-rated movie scene playing out in my head. "He had to have come up the drain. He's harmless but maybe there are more. I don't think I'm going to sleep well tonight."

She said, "Aren't crickets supposed to bring good luck?"

I blinked and smiled. "Oh, that's right. Hey, it's good luck for my new bathroom remodel."

The simple perception shift was enough to placate me. When I turned out the light that night, I did think of the sink skier sliding on the porcelain slope. Then I reminded myself he'd arrived with good luck—and that what you believe matters most. That's the basis for this week's practice. No insects needed.

Why This Remedy Works

What we believe shapes our experience. Imbuing an object, a being, or even a thought with power, luck, or meaning changes how we think. That's how a touchstone or talisman works. Like a ritual, the intention or significance we assign to almost anything can dispel anxiety and increase confidence. Whether crickets actually bring good luck is beside the point. As the remodel went forward, we encountered a few setbacks, but instead of going down the rabbit hole of angst and distress, I remembered my little friend. The cricket had become a sort of talisman and my thoughts about him were a touchstone. It would all work out.

How to Use This Remedy

Think of events in the past that are similar to my cricket story. Maybe help arrived at just the right moment and later you thought of the person as a guardian angel. Or perhaps as a kid you were given a lucky charm before a big school event, and because you performed well that time, you continued carrying it for good luck. You might wear a cross necklace as a symbol of your faith that reminds you you're safe in the hands of God. During my tenure as the president of a writing organization, I wore a sparkly duck brooch to remind me to let member strife roll away like water off a duck's back. Can you think of anything in your history that relates? What touchstones or talismans have you benefited from? Write about those.

_____

_____

_____

_____

_____

_____

What touchstone or talisman might help you now? Some people keep a Bible by their bedside and are calmed by reading a passage each night. Their faith in God's presence is their touchstone. Similarly, prayers for a loved one's health and happiness help them to "let go and let God." You might have another holy book or a particular author's or philosopher's words that bring you comfort. The poet Mary Oliver's thoughts read like dancing breezes that impart wisdom and joy—and if you believe they have the power to soothe you, they will.

Other ideas for touchstones or talismans:

- A relied-upon mantra you murmur to calm your racing mind.

- A short visualization. You see yourself boxing up distressing thoughts and putting them on a high shelf that requires a ladder to reach. Or, you shed your "backpack" that holds your regrets so that you feel lighter.

- Wearing a locket with the picture of a departed loved one whose strength you admired. The jewelry might serve as a reminder of the person's encouraging words or perhaps their courage and grit you strive to emulate.

- A "palm stone" to clutch. A cool, smooth stone of any kind may provide comfort. Or choose a crystal for its professed properties, i.e. smoky quartz is said to clear the mind of negative thoughts and self-doubt.

- A toad that visits your porch most evenings might come to represent your own strength in solitude, quiet introspection, and self-possessed acceptance of life as it is. (No matter the creature you greet as a touchstone or talisman, consider what it represents to you personally before looking up its symbolic meanings in books or online. Your intuitive responses may provide insight.)

Your task this week is to choose a touchstone or talisman. Experiment until you find one that feels right. These can be specific objects, thoughts, or beings you know or bring to mind. Give the item, thought, or creature significance. What does this mean to and for you? Write down your intentions. Practice with the touchstone or talisman. Write about your experience.

_____

_____

_____

RUMINATION REMEDIES

Remedy 28

Tidy Up

Initial Notes

A person's physical environment often reflects their interior one. Surrounding ourselves with physical items offers insulation but also closes us in. An extreme hoarder ends up with little room to move or expand. As the clutter builds up all around, s/he becomes limited to small pathways. Similarly, our minds can fill with emotional "clutter." Well-worn thought paths dig us into ruts in how we view ourselves, other people, and the world. Just as a hoarded home might isolate us in shame or embarrassment and become physically unsafe, narrow neural pathways limit connections to a wider network of creativity and possibility as well as harm our health.

Imagine a home filled with towering stacks of old newspapers rife with bad news and fearful outlooks. Similarly, a mind that holds old fears, resentments, worries, and regrets is like a maze of dreadful headlines. Thankfully, escape *is* possible.

There's something about a clear table that feels fresh and makes room for something new and different. Ditto drawers and cupboards emptied after years of filling. Even whole garages and spare bedrooms, when given a clean sweep, open the door to possibilities. This time, we'll tidy up.

Why This Remedy Works

Physical clutter increases physical stress, creates confusion, and decreases decisiveness. If our visual cortex is confused by overwhelming environmental cues, we're distracted and lose focus.[1,2,3] All of these contribute to mental chaos. Stress hormones affect outlook and can trigger negative thinking. If we're indecisive and can't concentrate, we're more likely to berate ourselves, wish we'd have done better, or relate our inconsistency to an existing emotional hurt, even without realizing, and run its related rumination reels. For older adults in particular, decluttering enhances feelings of control over one's life.[4] In short, clearing physical space clears a path to more positive thinking.

How to Use This Remedy

First, let's draw a few parallels between physical and mental clutter. Take time to reflect upon and record your unique experiences of these comparisons.

Physical hoarders hang onto possessions regardless of usefulness or value. This may connect with perfectionism, anxiety, trauma, or regret.[5] What mental clutter are you clinging to that is no longer helpful to you? Consider sayings you have lived by, such as: "Always do your best," or "Never give up," or "Don't be a quitter," and how these might connect to behavior and ruminative episodes and thinking styles you've identified while using this workbook. For example, if your rumination is frequently filled with guilt, is it because you're judging past behavior as not your best. We can learn from past mistakes or wish we'd have done things differently based on what we know now and didn't then, but there's no changing the past. Or, is your learned belief to "never give up"? Persistence is helpful but not when applied obsessively or when a situation becomes hurtful. Learn a new saying: "Know when to quit." What's your mental clutter?

___

___

___

___

___

___

___

Those with a hoarding disorder feel intensely attached to physical objects and believe discarding them will cause great distress.[6] Do you have strong feelings or areas of thinking that you judge as wrong or too painful to let go? Some say they continue to ruminate over a relationship because it's the only connection they have left to that person.[7] Letting go may feel like abandoning their role as a mother, friend, sister, etc. (which feels "wrong"). What thoughts are you attached to?

_____

_____

_____

To work toward releasing these unhelpful ways of thinking, you can begin by setting intentions to support letting go of physical clutter.

Write several sentences that affirm your decisions to tidy up. I've included two generalized examples for you to consider as you come up with statements that are more specific to you. As you did in Remedy 26, choose words that indicate positive momentum forward. Change to universal "you" statements if that feels more empowering for you.

Examples:

- As I clear this physical space, my perspective is also clearing my mind.
- I'm revealing new pathways and possibilities inside and out.

_____

_____

_____

_____

_____

_____

Set aside specific time to clear physical clutter. Begin with areas that you can clear in under an hour. Work up to larger, more complex projects as needed. Consider also *where* you'll start. Tidying unkempt space in the bedroom, such as your night table and its drawers, can promote a calmer space for improved sleep.

Write about the first space you chose to clear. Do you see a parallel between your physical and mental being? Expand upon your insights as you continue this process. How do you feel after organizing and clearing space? One man said he felt suddenly free and empowered toward new hobbies. Continue to journal on this activity over time.

_____

_____

_____

_____

_____

_____

_____

_____

_____

_____

_____

_____

Remedy 29

In Flow

Initial Notes

As a long-time author, the act of writing gets me in a state of intense yet sometimes effortless concentration. It's a state of being that was termed "flow" by researcher, Mihaly Csikszentmihalyi, in 1975. A flow state is different from "going with the flow," which means adapting to circumstances without resisting them. Have you ever gotten lost in some complex and meaningful task? My guess is yes, and you've experienced flow.

A friend of mine grows grapes and makes wine. From clipping back vines to seeing grapes spring forth, to the labor of harvesting and crushing, to the taste of his award-winning blends on the tip of his tongue, he enjoys flow states in the nurturing and vinting. Another friend has spent years perfecting her performance at a sport she has loved since her teen years: equine barrel racing. Her gleaming, dinner plate-sized belt buckle trophies are tangible proof of her flow states while in the saddle and feeling at one with her horse.

Finding flow at work or in hobbies and creative pursuits has many benefits. This week, you'll evaluate your personal flow states and make a practice of getting into flow.

Why This Remedy Works

Experiencing flow helps with negative thinking because it protects against depression and burnout, both of which are associated with rumination.[1] Even in those for whom anxiety and rumination are typical, the ability to enjoy flow ameliorates those tendencies.[2] In short, by losing ourselves in the moment, we gain peace.[3]

How to Use This Remedy

Flow is found in doing activities that are both challenging and for which you have developed a level of skill.[4] Where have you experienced flow? Start by thinking of things you enjoy or are naturally good at. For example, I was always drawn to writing and had some skill from the moment I put pen to paper and realized the power of the pen. I also love gardening and can lose myself as much in the dreaming up of outcomes as I can in the hands-on chores. I get lost in reading about different plants, how they found their way to the U.S., studying their needs, and contemplating whether they'll grow in my yard. Reflect upon *your* life. When, where, and in what have *you* lost all track of time in the present? Whether work or hobby, record those times now.

_____

_____

_____

_____

Let's consider what's vital to get you into flow.

Trigger positive emotions. Upbeat music, a walk outdoors, a laughy friend, a funny movie or story, or a much-loved pet can lift your mood and trigger positive feelings. Whatever it is that makes you smile or feel satisfaction, do it. Go back to the photos you took for Remedy 10, *Cherished Evidence*. Do you remember your satisfaction, contentment, or pride in a job well done? Comb through your memories for any positive emotions and savor them. Upbeat moods inhibit self-consciousness, which is an element of flow. Negative emotions and worry can inhibit the state.[5]

Nurture talent or skill. Focus on an area where you have some level of expertise and skill already. The idea is to strike a balance between challenge and skill. Practicing at something we know about and adding a challenging element can be the sweet spot to achieve flow. If you've knitted lots of simple hats, for example, the task might have become too easy to truly activate flow. Adding a new technique or making a more complex hat style could be the next-level challenge to get you into a flow state.[5]

Develop intrinsic motivation. The flow state is considered "autotelic." The term comes from two Greek words: autos (self) and telos (end or goal), meaning the activity itself becomes the goal. The value is in the doing. For this reason, it helps to choose activities you enjoy.

Go back to the list you made above, add any additional ideas, then choose an activity and make a practice of getting into a state of flow. Set a time, enhance your mood with positive-emotion triggers as needed, and then get started. Don't neglect activities you used to love, even from childhood.

 Additional Tips & Techniques

While losing yourself in something meaningful is beneficial, it's important to also take care of yourself. I've become so adept at entering a flow state when I'm writing that I have found myself "waking up" from the process with hurting joints and intense thirst. That's not optimal so I've built in reminders to take a few minutes break every hour or so. You might need to employ a similar tactic.

Sometimes, using a prop can help you get into flow. After my move to a smaller home, I realized putting on an apron enhanced my decluttering sessions. The apron prompted a shift. I would put down other pressing tasks or worries and pick up the act of sorting, trashing, or giving away. Using a timer freed me to work for set periods, which motivated focus. While I wouldn't say I *enjoy* decluttering, I did lose myself in the task such that the timer sounding surprised me. Is there a prop you can use to shift gears and get into flow?

You can also use flow for acute situations. If you awaken early or have trouble getting to sleep, for example, try abandoning the effort. Get into flow instead. Pick up your chosen activity and have at it. You might lose the sleep you were losing anyway but you'll also lose yourself—and gain the benefits of a break from painful rumination.

This week, practice getting into flow states. Then write about your experience. Notice how your negative thinking drops in relation to your flow sessions.

_____

_____

_____

_____

Remedy 30

A Sigh of Relief

Initial Notes

Years ago, when one of my adult sons estranged from our family, rumination became a constant. My mind incessantly raced. *Why did he do this*? *How could this happen*? *What might the future hold*? I was devastated and miserable yet determined to carry on. As I applied myself to my daily life, another constant became apparent: heavy sighs.

Louds sighs broadcasted my arrival to any room, punctuated my rest periods, and announced my shift to any new activity. Those sighs were prominent and troubling. They were proof of just how far into the dumps I'd dropped. My other adult children noticed and commented, which made me feel even worse.

Irritated and wanting to model strength, I judged the sighing as a sign of weakness and tried to stop. Whenever I caught one of those long, desperate sighs escaping me, I gritted my teeth and carried on, but I also worried I'd never get past the hurt. Each sigh seemed to advertise my failure.

Too bad I didn't know then what I know now. My involuntary sighs were actually a natural healing response. Sighs were my body's way to cope with the horrible hurt and anxiety coursing through my nervous system.

At this point in the workbook, you've read repeatedly that what we believe influences us. This experience is another example. I denigrated my involuntary sighs as proof of weakness and beat myself up. If I had instead seen my involuntary sighs as an innate healing tool, I would have been amazed by the body's natural wisdom. Then I could have purposefully worked with those sighs to increase my well-being and better cope.

Why This Remedy Works

We all sigh. There are important physiological reasons, including maximum expansion of the lungs, which prevents the progressive collapse of the tiny air sacs called alveoli.[1] Babies sigh spontaneously every few minutes. Adult sighs are typically less frequent but still occur spontaneously and regularly.[1] Where this gets interesting is that, according to research, anxiety and traumatic events often precede a syndrome of irrepressible sighing.[2]

While our breaths occur with regularity, the number and depth will shift depending on our activity or state. When we talk, eat, laugh, or cry, our breathing adapts. If we're on the edge of our seat at a movie, we involuntarily hold our breath in anticipation or fear. If we're concentrating hard or feeling anxious, we take fewer breaths. A sigh resets our breath—and calms the central nervous system, which affects how we feel.[3, 4, 5, 6, 7, 8] When we feel calm, our breath reflects that because there's a natural interplay between our emotional state and our breathing. The converse is also true. We can be purposeful with our breath and positively influence how we feel. Or, we can work against it, inhibiting the body's innate wisdom, and negatively judging ourselves such that our breathing reacts in anxious patterns that cause physiological distress and further hurt us.

Using the breath as an effective tool to calm ourselves can take many forms. Physiological sighing, also known as cyclic sighing, is an excellent form. In fact, in a published 2023 study that tested several breathing techniques, those who practiced cyclic sighs showed the most improvement in physical and mental well-being. What is more, the overall positive effects increased as the study went on, suggesting that breathwork practice and, in particular, cyclic sighing, has lasting benefits.[9]

How to Use This Remedy

Start with a short practice of two or three cyclic sighs once or twice a day. Before breakfast or before going to bed, for example. Here's the basic method:

Inhale once through the nose, followed by another, shorter inhale through the nose. Then exhale in a long sigh through the mouth. Make sure the exhalation is longer than the combined inhales.

The practice may at first feel awkward. Remember, that first breath in through the nose is long and smooth, followed by a quick breath in. Then make your exhalation longer than those combined. Counting as you breathe helps. Try reading the following to yourself as you breathe.

Inhale one, two, three, four, five...
Inhale one...
Exhale one, two, three, four, five, six, seven.

Once you're used to the practice, use it whenever you feel stressed. When your inner voice amps up, catastrophizes, or loops on negativity, take a breather (excuse the pun). You might as well benefit while you're sitting in traffic (traff-*ick*) or when a companion makes you late.

REMEDY 30: A Sigh of Relief

As you make physiological sighing part of your daily routine and turn to the sighs whenever you're stressed, pay attention to your overall mood. Note how the sighs work to calm you in moments of acute distress. What do you notice about how your body feels? How did your posture change? Describe how your mind shifts. Write about your experience.

Remedy 31

Learning Curve, Body in Mind

Initial Notes

Most of the exercises since the last *Learning Curve* section, and many throughout the workbook, called for action. You were required to move, speak, or take other deliberative actions. The actions weren't always directly related to rumination. For decades, the scientific world has all but divorced the workings of the brain from the body. In recent years, marrying the mind back to the rest of the body (embodied cognition) has been embraced, but connecting mind and body is not new. In 1916, Margaret Floy Washburn, the first woman to earn a doctorate in psychology, thought the connection was vital to human well-being. However, scientists that followed her ushered in other ideas that buried hers.[1]

Why Embodiment Works

Learning is attached to and affected by what we do and say, the gestures we make, and our interactions in and with the world around us. From our earliest ages, we're handed a toy as a parent narrates their action: "Here's your toy." Or we're asked, "Where's the doggie?" and are encouraged to point. Movement is naturally inherent in learning.[1] Combine that idea with the knowledge that purposeful action calms anxiety, and it's easy to understand why therapeutic trauma-informed work often includes the somatic.

Some of the action- and movement-based practices in the workbook include direct links to your thinking. The movement and metaphor from Remedy 26, *Solvitur Ambulando*, is one example. Others are less directly connected but no less helpful. Movement supports integration. Taking action, whether it's tidying up, journaling, or whispering your troubles to a doll (Remedies 28, 23, and 24), gives the mind a break from its overprocessing. And the act of doing one thing makes other things feel doable. One accomplishment feeds confidence for another—even when unrelated.

Take a moment to reflect upon what part movement has played in your life. Previously, have you considered its impact on your cognition and outlook? As you've progressed through the workbook, how has movement impacted your relationship with your thoughts?

_____

_____

_____

_____

_____

Measure Your Progress

Which of the skills covered in Remedies 23–30 have you experimented with? Below, you'll find each of the techniques listed. To the left, check off each of the techniques you've tried.

Review your notes and reflect upon each experience. Run through the steps again if that feels necessary. Then, using a scale of 0–10 where ten means super helpful and zero means not helpful all, write the number that best represents your experience with each technique (on the line to the right).

_____ **23: Pour it Out** (*Journaling for helpful insight.*) _____

_____ **24: Say it to the Dolls** (*Releasing your worries.*) _____

_____ **25: Normalize** (*You're not so different or alone.*) _____

_____ **26:** *Solvitur ambulando* (*Physical and metaphorical momentum.*) _____

_____ **27: Touchstones and Talismans** (*Symbols of positive perception.*) _____

_____ **28: Tidy Up** *(External order for internal order.)* _____

_____ **29: In Flow** *(Losing track of yourself and time.)* _____

_____ **30: A Sigh of Relief** *(Using a natural form of stress-reducing breathwork.)* _____

Catch Up or Toss

Now is the time to return to and try any techniques you skipped or didn't fully attend to. Also consider any *Additional Tips and Techniques* boxes you neglected. Rate or re-rate techniques as needed.

What Didn't Help?

Reflect on any exercises that weren't helpful to you. Pointing out what didn't work for you helps discharge negative energy and let it go. As needed, use the lines here for that purpose.

_____

_____

_____

Favorites So Far

Using your ratings of Remedies 23–30, note the tools you found most helpful. Consider why these worked. What did you like about them? How easy were they to implement and remember?

Reflecting here will provide insight into the best times for you to experiment as well as how to make the techniques more your own. After journaling about your favorites, use the last block of lines in this *Learning Curve* to record the titles of your favorites among Remedies 23–30.

_____

_____

_____

My Go-Tos

Remedy 32

Tune in and Tune Out

Initial Notes

One reason parents give babies sensory toys is to keep them occupied. They hang a busy board with spinners, latches, doors, and mirrors inside the crib. Or they might give toddlers a busy book that features bumpy, soft, or crinkly inserts, and flip-up parts. The items can offer learning engagement during the night or at times when quiet is needed. The child tunes *in* to these sensory stimuli and tunes *out* their inner urges (boredom, fear, hunger, or loneliness). Adults are not all that different. The trick is to find and purposely turn to what best engages our senses.

When babies interact with a busy board, they naturally gravitate to an option or two. One repeatedly activates a sound maker; another likes the soft feel of velvet. A mirror might best engage another. Adults, too, have sensory go-tos. That's why one parent, whose adult son gives him grief, blasts *AC-DC* tunes on his way to work [1] while another might roll the window down, relish the warmth of sunlight on his arm, and enjoy the feel of the breeze. Engaging the senses pulls us in. We tune *in* to the sound or feel (or sight, touch, or smell) and tune *out* our inner turmoil.

Why This Remedy Works

As with the grounding techniques discussed in Remedy 15, engaging the senses shifts focus to the present moment. When your mind is in overdrive and you purposely turn to a particular sensory channel, you train your brain to pair that catalyst with breaking the chains of rumination. With practice, you create a habit where the mind shifts more automatically from its overactive loop.

There's wisdom in busy boards and books with their variety of sensory offerings. While it works to engage one sense, don't neglect the feast of a smorgasbord. I first wrote about the full engagement of senses required in baking bread from scratch in a 2020 blog post at my website to help parents with estranged adult children. The all-in nature of the activity helped calm my emotional distress.[2]

Breadmaking is both science and art, engaging full attention. Shifts in room temperature affect rising. A flour's moisture content varies by flour type, making measurements imprecise and requiring keen senses to get it right. In the tactile act of kneading, the dough's appearance, elasticity, and texture all inform the baker. Then there's the thud of the dough as you pat it against the board or plop it into the bowl. Add the slightly acrid smell of raw yeast, the tantalizing aroma as bread bakes, and your own squeal of delight when pulling the crusty loaf from the oven, and the process is a sensory feast. That I turned to this daily during an especially troubling time made it an encompassing sensory go-to that obliterated rumination.

Gardening is similarly engaging. I've grown some amazing flowers, fruits, and vegetables during my most stressful periods. The warmth of sunlight, the rich smell of the earth and blooms, bright pops of color, the feel of moist dirt, and the sounds of birds singing provide an all-in distraction.

People who enjoy crafts relish in the textures of fabric scraps and paper, the scent of potpourri, the aesthetic arrangements that treat the eye, and the din of background music or the chit-chat of working alongside other crafters. What all-senses activities do *you* enjoy?

For me, breadmaking became an engaging daily ritual. You'll remember the power of rituals from Remedy 20. Drawing from other remedies, here are more reasons why an all-in sensory go-to works:

- *Cognitive load.* The more sensory input the brain processes at once, the less cognitive bandwidth is left to overthink.

- *Enhanced presence.* The more senses you engage at once, the more present you'll be, removing mental time travel of (past) regret and (future) worry.

- *Nervous system regulation.* Sensory input can reduce stress hormones such as cortisol and activate your parasympathetic nervous system for a calming response. Engaging multiple senses at once forges neural highways leading to calm and weakens the byways of rumination.

- *Disruption.* The strong stimulus of multi-sensory engagement increases disruptor power.

Using several senses at once multiplies their power via strong, diverse input to the brain. This reinforces parasympathetic activation (rest and digest). In keeping with the benefit of metaphors (Remedy 26), think of using several senses at once like a great wall of powerful peacemakers advancing forward like soldiers to neutralize the ruminative strength of niggling (fight or flight) stress-stirrers.

 ## How to Use This Remedy

Experiment with your senses and find your go-tos. Does music move you? Build a soundtrack that gets your happy juices flowing. Or choose one song and play it daily as a ritual. You might enjoy textures, so petting your fur baby is a convenient go-to (and s/he will love you back). Or perhaps you choose a soft blanket or a silky scarf. Some years ago, I purged my closet of denim and other woven fabrics, opting for luscious velvets and stretchy knits. It just *feels* right.

Perhaps you add scents to your home, arrange colorful throws and sofa pillows, or in some other way engage your senses. The idea is to identify ways to stimulate the senses … and then purposely engage them whenever negative thinking begins. Also, experiment with pre-emptive measures such as a ritualized song you play, or a specific scent you keep on hand. I use essential oils in humidifiers that I can activate with the flip of a switch, keep my poodles with their strokable soft fur near, and have minty gum at the ready so my taste buds become a path to peace.

Write down ideas that immediately come to mind. Then, use the prompts to come up with more.

_____

_____

_____

_____

_____

Which scents soothe you?

_____

_____

_____

_____

What sounds do you love?

_____

_____

_____

_____

What enjoyable activities engage several senses at once?

_____

_____

_____

_____

What sight, smell, touch, and sound changes can you bring to your environment?

_____

_____

_____

_____

Is there a soothing taste you can add? Or perhaps a thought-disruptive taste, like sour lemons or tart candy.

_____

_____

_____

_____

Over the next week or so, assemble a few sensory peacemakers and experiment with them. Then write about your experiences. How did these cause a shift? Which ones will you keep around and turn to often?

_____

_____

_____

_____

_____

_____

_____

_____

_____

_____

"The crust was brown and crisp, the crumb snowy white,
and the fragrance filled the room like music."
—*Eliza Acton* (1799–1859)

Remedy 33

P-R-O-C-E-E-D

Initial Notes

Did you know the brain uses two routes to alert you to stimuli and trigger your response? One is a short subcortical route to your brain's amygdala, a small structure that registers fear and danger. This prompts quick reactions without detailed processing—perfect for emergencies. The other route sends information on a longer path to your cerebral cortex for subjective analysis, interpretation, and critical response. Both routes start at the thalamus, a structure deep inside your brain that's sometimes referred to as a relay station, because it gathers external and internal stimuli and transmits information.

Obviously, not all stimuli are critical to life and death. The trouble is, when your thinking activates your fight-or-flight response, you may misinterpret the urgency. Whether you react in ways that involve other people, or you only torment yourself with catastrophizing and self-recrimination, your brain's short route makes matters worse. Here, you'll learn an acronym to deactivate the red alert and take advantage of your brain's longer, more thoughtful route.

Why This Remedy Works

The familiar "count to 10" rule applies. When you're aware of high-alert activation, you can purposely pause and give your brain's more logical responses time to engage.

 How to Use This Remedy

The first step is to know what happens when your thoughts trigger danger and activate your central nervous system alarms. That means catching yourself when your mind gets going in a negative direction. Also notice your bodily responses. Do your fists clench? Does your throat or chest constrict? Do your brows furrow? Does your breath catch and become shallow? Do your shoulders grow tight? You may immediately recall what happens in those tense moments just from reading this. If so, take notes. Then, during the next few days, continue to notice your physiological reactions and add them to your list. Your bodily reactions are another pathway to awareness.

Write about your physical reactions. And please, *give yourself grace*. Awareness becomes easier with practice.

_____

_____

_____

_____

_____

_____

_____

_____

_____

REMEDY 33: P-R-O-C-E-E-D

Once you know yourself better, you're ready to PROCEED. I created the acronym to help myself and others move out of red-alert mode and relax into critical thinking and a sensible response. When you find your mind running wild and dragging your physiology with it, follow these steps:

P: *Pause.* You've noticed your thoughts knotting. Tell yourself: *Pause.* Make the purposeful choice of bringing your mind to rest.

R: *Relax.* Use the power of your breath to calm your nervous system. With a cyclic sigh or simply slowing and deepening your breaths ... *relax*.

O: *Observe.* Tune in to your physical body. If your fists are clenched, relax them. If your brows are furrowed, release the tension. Roll tight shoulders and let them droop. Let your tongue loll. Observe how it feels to *relax*.

C: *Critical thinking.* With the PRO (pause, relax, observe) period, you gave your mind time to access its logic and reason. You'll note your thoughts may have slowed. Use a soothing inner voice to acknowledge this step. *You've made it. You're here now. You're okay.*

E: *Examine.* Here's where you'll use your critical thinking to take a closer look at your thoughts, what triggered them, and whether they're accurate. Ask yourself: *What's the content?* Are you catastrophizing, worrying about the future, or holding regret? Then, use challenge questions such as: *Is that true? Is it certain that will happen?* Confront absolutes in your self-talk such as *always*, *never*, and *won't*. If you're re-playing a troubling incident, hug yourself (sensory power of touch). Using a kind inner or outer voice, gently acknowledge how much this incident hurt or upset you. Tell yourself: *You're safe now. You're going to be okay.*

E: *Elevate.* Here's where future worries can be shifted to better possible outcomes. You can purposefully let go and let God, put your trust in a higher power, or recognize that your "crystal ball" needs adjusting. Forgive yourself. Regrets can be seen as part of the human condition. Acknowledge what you wish you'd done differently, recognize that mistakes/regrets prompt learning, and plan for future change. For this step, affirmations help. More about that below.

D: *Decide.* The final step is to take charge of what's next. With the crisis averted, you have no reason to return to it. Choose to proceed with your previously planned day. You might also journal about what derailed you (Remedy 23), practice earthing or grounding (Remedies 21 and 15), or engage your senses (Remedy 32). Tell yourself: *You're in charge.*

Additional Tips and Techniques

Consider whether the fear that's registering from your thinking needs additional action or processing. Sometimes, thoughts that trigger a fight-or-flight response genuinely alert us to danger. A person who feels stuck in an abusive home or work relationship may ruminate, but just as ruminating doesn't help (and perhaps adds to an existing sense of powerlessness), neither does staying stuck. The same could be true of continuing to reach out to a family member who is hurtful to you because you're told you should. PROCEED, with its calming and reflective elements, can provide insight into what may be a real and present danger in your life.

PROCEED this week, and in the future, as needed. Reflection allows for insight and adaptation. Write about your experience and also create affirmations that "elevate" your mood and thinking per the second "E" in PROCEED. By reviewing your notes from weeks one and two, as well as what has shifted as you've proceeded through the workbook, you can make your affirmations relevant and helpful to your present self. Here are some general examples using the supportive "you" format (change to I if that feels more powerful):

- You're using logic and reason for positive change.

- You easily release triggers of the past and embrace peace now and in the future.

- You're growing into your wisest self.

_____

_____

_____

_____

_____

Remedy 34

Bend Your Ear?

Initial Notes?
At some point, you've probably had someone figuratively "bend" your ear with a drawn-out story. Now bend your own—literally. Gentle pressure, massage, and folding of the ear can stimulate the vagus nerve for relaxation benefits.

Why This Remedy Works
The vagus nerve is associated with your parasympathetic nervous system, meaning that good vagal tone increases associated responses of calm and resilience to stress. Much research exists about stimulating the vagus nerve via the ears for better sleep, increased heart rate variability, migraine relief, and improvements in mood.[1, 2] Here, we'll use a generalized ear pressure and massage routine. A positive side effect may be that your face looks lifted. That's because the fascia in and around the ear connect with the muscles in the face. Massage can release tension, producing a softer, more uplifted appearance.

 ## Additional Tips and Techniques

> To find out more about the ear as a system with acupressure points corresponding to areas of the body, look up the term "auriculotherapy." Acupuncture has long relied upon meridian points in the ears. Auriculotherapy is similar but without needles. With some working knowledge, you can manipulate the points on your own. Additionally, many scientific studies

focus on electrical stimulation of the auricle branch of the vagus nerve. Even the field of cardiology has conducted recent studies using ear clips that provide electrical stimulation, and physicians are excited about the prospects.[3] At home, a TENS unit can be used.[4] Or look into the many consumer-direct devices available for vagus nerve stimulation. These devices are generally considered safe. However, some health conditions warrant extra caution or make electrical stimulation ill-advised. Check with your doctor.

How to Use This Remedy

Try this routine a couple of times a day. Pinpoint times when you may need the most help, such as bedtime. Use at critical overthinking times too. Be gentle in your technique. With practice, you may find that your ears are less sensitive and respond well to more pressure or manipulation. Do not tug, press, bend or fold to the point of causing pain. Here, I'm including my own routine. In time, you may find that you alter the order of the steps in a way that feels natural to you.

1. Gently press your palms over your ears and, with a slightly upward or circular motion, press and release several times.

2. Lightly cup your ears by placing your thumbs underneath your earlobes and your fingers over the tops of your ears. Using gentle pressure, fold the tops and bottoms of your ears inward and hold for a few seconds. You can also try using a gentle pumping motion.

3. Using your thumb and index finger, gently massage and tug downward on your earlobes. Repeat 3–5 times. Then "walk" your thumb and index finger upward along your outer ear.

4. Massage the tops of your ears in a rhythmic, upward motion.

5. With your index fingers, gently press and massage the tragus, the small flap in front of your ear canal.

6. Move your fingertips to the area behind your ears and gently massage, sliding your fingers down behind your earlobes and toward your jaw. Repeat.

7. Linger your touch on any sensitive areas that may be asking for additional care.

8. Finish with a body stretch and yawn.

Write about your experience using this massage technique. Over the next week, notice and record changes in your ears' sensitivity as well as overall relaxation response, how this helps at different times of the day, and any changes in your thinking patterns or sleep.

RUMINATION REMEDIES

Remedy 35

Worst-Case Scenario

Initial Notes

"What if something happens to him?" In my early 30s, I remember expressing my biggest fear to a dear friend: That something would happen to my husband, and I'd be left with five children to raise alone.

At the time, I was still reeling from my mother's sudden death. The shock of life's uncertainty had shaken my world. My husband, who was also grieving, had become distant. He was preoccupied with growing his business to support our expanded family. Life had gotten difficult, and I felt alone.

"Well, what if?" My friend shrugged.

I blundered ahead, describing the story my worried mind conjured up: a catastrophic landscape left me penniless and homeless. My barefoot children, their solemn, gaunt faces smudged with dirt, clung to ragged soft toys with the stuffing spilling out.

My friend wasn't buying it.

"You're not going to let that happen," she said. "You'd do whatever it took, and there's a lot you could do."

I blinked, suddenly rapt but still doubtful. "Like what?"

"You could rent space on your property to store RVs," she offered. "And how about do bookkeeping for some of your husband's contractor friends?"

She was right, of course. I might have felt helpless, but I wasn't. Her suggestions were logical. In running my husband's business, I'd learned a lot. "I could do their safety programs, too," I said in a sudden mind shift. "I've learned the ins and outs of workman's compensation insurance, and the programs and paperwork required in California's strict employee protection climate."

"See?" She shrugged again. "And if none of that works, there's always your writing," she said, stirring laughter in us both. At the time, we were young mothers, trying our hand at writing and discovering how competitive and dismally paying a business it could be.

While my "what if" had formed insurmountable mountains, my friend had challenged my thoughts with realistic, solution-based possibilities. She was right. If push came to shove, I'd be motivated by my big *why*, to keep my children safe (my "Wi-Fi") and shift into forward gear. That shift is what this remedy is all about.

Why This Remedy Works

Frequently, people seize upon a what-if scenario and then imagine the worst. One horrible thought rolls into the next like rocks in an avalanche. Next thing you know, you're buried in fear. Cutting through the rubble to clearly identify the fears, challenge them, and then shift to solutions puts you back in control.

How to Use This Remedy

When you're ruminating in a worst-case scenario fashion, pretend you're a wise friend, use the universal you, and ask yourself:

- What exactly are you afraid of?

Use the lines to answer the question. Add details as I did above. The thought of my children in sorry straits provided buy-in to my friend's challenge and suggested solutions.

_____

_____

_____

_____

_____

My friend reminded me of my strength and my options. You can remind yourself to step back into *your* wise self and consider *your* options. Whatever worst-case scenario you're imagining, move on to choices that fit your abilities. You do have options to help yourself. Does someone you love no longer have room for you in his/her life? Your fear may be that they never will, that you're unlikeable, and perhaps you will end up all alone. As my friend would say, "*Well, what if?*" Remind yourself who has, and does, like you—and that being alone isn't the end of the world. Call it "solitude," and you've reframed the status into something good. Then, with your fear identified and appropriate reminders in place, brainstorm solutions. For example, if you're lonely, you can join activity clubs, do volunteer work, or find support groups. You were liked in the past and you'll be liked in the future. Find people who understand and pull you up from the paralysis of catastrophizing.

Just as my fear required me to look at my Wi-Fi (to keep my children safe), access yours in relation to the fear. That's your pivoting point, which requires accepting that the worst *could* happen and, if it did (or has), you can trust yourself to find options and live forward anyway.

Write your brainstormed solutions below.

Additional Tips and Techniques

With entrenched worst-case-scenario catastrophizing, it can help to consider also how likely it is that what you fear will actually happen. That puts a step in the middle and expands my friend's challenge. So, the three steps are:

- What *exactly* are your fears?

- Are these fears likely to happen? How likely?

- If these fears materialize, how might you respond for the best (your options)?

_____

_____

_____

_____

Remedy 36

Your B-F-F

Initial Notes

A shallow pond on my property teems with tadpoles each spring. When the Great Blue Herons grow weary of standing over gopher holes waiting for movement, they wade in. Even in the water, they're statuesque, perfectly still so their prey doesn't notice them. So, why can't I get a good photo? No matter how stealthily I creep around the corner of the house behind the tall bushes some 500-feet away, as soon as I raise my head, those sharp-eyed herons raise theirs. Herons have amazing depth perception and macro-vision to scope aquatic life through wavy water. They shift in an instant to binocular vision to zoom in on me in the distance.[1] Then, lickety-split, they fly off to confound some other hopeful photographer.

Human eyesight is about three times less detailed than the Great Blue Heron. Our eyes aren't built to so deftly shift our visual perception, but assuming the distance of a metaphorical bird's-eye view helps us escape a negative thinking spin cycle. *How?* One way is to think like a friend. In Remedy 35, I told you about a friend who challenged my catastrophic paralysis and moved me toward solutions. Her outsider perspective of me and my life allowed the distance of big-picture insight. Here, you'll step into the persona of a wise friend because, just as fresh eyes make things look new (Remedy 17), a friend's broader view sheds new light.

Why This Remedy Works

It's easy to give someone else advice. Think of watching sports where we holler at players to take a shot or block one. From the spectator's vantage point, we easily see a bigger picture than those inside the game can. They're too close to the issue—just like when we're lost in the forest of our own thinking.

How to Use This Remedy

Next time you find your thoughts heading south, assume the role of a spectator friend. Look at the bigger picture. Challenge your thinking. Remind yourself of your strengths and offer encouragement from the sidelines.

Rumination whips the mind into negative spirals that suck us deeper. If one person is critical of us or our work, we might begin to believe everyone is. If we fail once, we imagine we'll fail at everything. We grow hopeless. In such despair, our whole selves are affected—body, mind, and spirit. This makes us more stressed and sensitive. In such a state, we might magnify constructive criticism to the point of seeing ourselves as irredeemable. Then we're more vulnerable to abuse. So, if someone we care about tells us we're a bad parent (or a lousy sister, an inattentive friend, a lazy coworker….), we take the words to heart. This can be especially true when the circumstances are reminiscent of unhealthy aspects from past relationships. A loyal friend would see the big picture and set us straight. *Be your own best friend.*

Notice comprehensive judgments in your thinking. "I never" or "I always" are clues you're treading into murky, ruminative waters. Ask yourself:

- Is that really true? (For example, are you really a "failure" because you didn't see that coming? Because you failed *this time*? Because you forgot a meeting? Because…)

Borrow from Your Turnaround (Remedy 2) and use the technique here. Tell yourself, just as a true-blue friend would, that you don't forget your meetings every day and that everyone misses a date at some point. Then, just as a friend would, consider the possible reasons why you forgot, e.g., you were physically or emotionally exhausted, were distracted, or just too busy and, in being human, you're not superhuman.

No matter what the content, if self-doubt, worry, or regret creeps in and begins to spin, remind yourself of your value the way a friend would. Even go to the mirror and talk to your reflection. Or, close your eyes and see your wiser self as s/he assures the distressed and frightened version of you that:

- You succeeded before. You can succeed again.

- You overcame that obstacle (name it). This is just another one you will get over, around, or through.

- While it's true that you have made mistakes, you have also done good. (Name a few ways. Think back as far as you need to.) Focus on those. It's the wiser you that you're aiming to emulate.

Remember, wherever you go, you're with yourself. So, you might as well be your own best friend. Assume a friendly vantage point. Challenge faulty thinking and be kind to yourself—your oldest friend.

Use the lines to prepare for this technique by recognizing your strengths and your values, and bolstering your self-worth. Reflect upon obstacles you have overcome in the past. Also record what strengths, skills, and personality traits you embodied and utilized for these triumphs.

_____

_____

_____

_____

_____

Instead of beating ourselves up for real or imagined failures, it's important to celebrate the good we have done. What are you proud of? Think of times you maintained your values or goodwill despite adversity or in the face of unkindness. What does your loving inner friend see in you? Write down what comes to mind.

_____

_____

_____

_____

_____

We have all received compliments that made us feel good. Think of several things people have recognized you for. Consider and record why these compliments encouraged you.

Additional Tips and Techniques

We can also gain insight from what doesn't settle well with us. If your thoughts stray to endorsements or adulation that bring any sort of discomfort, record them here with an asterisk or in some other way mark them as separate. Reflect upon why the feedback wasn't encouraging to you. Sometimes, we become aware of vulnerable areas or discover hurts we've been protecting. Be gentle with yourself. Seek support as needed. That's what you would tell a friend.

_____

_____

_____

_____

_____

_____

_____

_____

_____

"When I look at you, I see the soul's light
shining through the dust of the day."
—*Unknown, verse printed in 19th-century periodicals*

Remedy 37

Real Eyes for Peace

Initial Notes

On a hiking trip with restful views of gnarly barked trees, distant mountains, and sparkling lakes, I let out a long sigh and said of my eyes, which felt restored by nature, "These are my real eyes." Gone were the tight, strained orbs of my routine life. In this vista-rich landscape of varied views, my eyes relaxed. What's becoming clear via science is that we can use our "real eyes" to "realize" peace. That is, we can adjust how and what we look at to bring about a peaceful state. This exercise takes a broad view toward your well-being.

Why This Remedy Works

We don't typically consider our eyes part of our brain, but neuroscientist Andrew Huberman says that's exactly what they are. The eyes are part of the central nervous system and keep us alert to potential threats. When you see something stressful, like an emotionally triggering text, your pupils dilate, your lens position shifts to the center, and your visual field narrows. It's how your vision naturally responds to stressors, filtering out excess data to focus on the danger.[1] In our modern world of palm-held technology and cities that clutter and obstruct longer views, your eyes may be triggering biological stress responses even without the irritating incoming text (or whatever else irks you). The good news is you can dial down your stress responses by expanding your view, which Huberman says, "releases a mechanism in the brain stem involved in vigilance and arousal."[1] In other words, taking a broad view widened to expand your peripheral vision is like pushing stress's Off button.

How to Use This Remedy

First, consider how much time you spend on detailed up-close tasks, poring over paperwork, or viewing screens. In day-to-day life, it's easy to lose sight of your thirst for expansive and varied views. But drink in the longer view of an ocean sunset, watch the sun rising slowly over the horizon, or notice how the big blue sky stretches all around, and peace settles into your breath and bones. The play of dappled sunlight on the ground as you walk, the shapes of birds on wing high above, and the soft frill of a bloom on a bare branch against the bright sky brings similar peace.

How many long views do you find the time, energy, and space to take in daily? How varied are your vision fields? Do you even notice? Do you take breaks from the focused visual attention of close work such as reading or computer time, to look up and out at the space around you? Write your thoughts here.

_____

_____

_____

Once you've created awareness around your visual ruts, make a practice of purposefully seeing the world. Over the next several days, give yourself opportunities to notice the things around you. Lift your gaze to see into the distance, then focus on something close. If you go on a walk, sit on a patio, or stand at a window, notice what's near and far. Use your vision to outline shapes in the fore- and background, decipher layers in the greenery or rooftops, and notice the play of light. Even if you can't go outdoors, look about in this manner. Your eyes crave variety. Write about your visual playtime. How does this affect your mood and thoughts?

_____

_____

_____

_____

Next, in as open a space as you can conveniently get to, stand still and face forward. With your head even and your eyes fixed on a point several yards away, notice what comes into view in your peripheral vision. I'm always amazed to realize just how much I can make out on either side of me. Blink and look elsewhere, then try this again. Are you surprised? Do you feel more in touch?

_____

_____

_____

Finally, you may have heard of EMDR (Eye Movement Desensitization and Reprocessing). This therapy technique uses lateral eye movements to reduce distress responses associated with trauma. I'm not suggesting this as a substitute for formal therapy, but you probably never noticed that lateral eye movements occur naturally as you move forward in space. This fact provides additional depth to the metaphorical language from Remedy 26.

Lateral eye movements suppress the activation of the amygdala, which is a large part of our threat-detection system.[2] Quieting the amygdala relieves stress, and because these lateral eye movements naturally occur as we step forward, the idea of taking a walk to clear your head and decompress makes perfect sense. You could spend 10–20 seconds in a chair with your head still, moving your eyes rapidly from side-to-side to invoke a sense of calm.[3] Or, use Mother Nature's hack and take a walk. Journal about your experiences.

_____

_____

_____

_____

_____

_____

Remedy 38

Bust a Move

Initial Notes

The people I work with frequently describe their progress as "one step forward, two steps back." They often feel bad about themselves, saying they're "weak" as they're pulled back into emotional distress over hurtful relationships. In those moments, their struggle blinds them to their overall progress. With support they begin to feel stronger and start to realize that with every shuffle backward, they are able to move more quickly forward again. Less time is spent in the backslide. As awareness grows, so does their confidence. They're more motivated to purposely step toward healing and happiness.

One day, in an online member discussion group I was leading, an attendee used the "one step forward, two steps back" phrasing to describe her recent setback. That's when a savvy fellow participant wrote into the chat: "It's a dance! One step forward, two steps back."

Her words made me laugh. How we relate to our emotional experience *is* a dance. Just as a jaunty tune might lighten a dancer's feet, the idea of seeing our setbacks and progress as an actual dance adds springy energy to the heavy situations we deal with. As you learned in Remedy 26, movement as a metaphor for momentum brings results. Today's remedy lets you bust a dance move to bust free of negative thinking.

Why This Remedy Works

At its most basic, dance is exercise with benefits including mood improvement, lowered anxiety, and a boost to cognitive ability. When you dance, those benefits partner with others and boogie even more. Dancing brings a rise in self-reported quality of life and even improvements to interpersonal skills. Dancing engages your mind as you decide upon steps and practice them. Even short, spontaneous sessions elevate mood and reduce anxiety.[1] Dancing with others has additional perks. Interaction at classes or events and trusted touch in partnered dances increase well-being, enhance one's sense of identity, and provide a feeling of kinship. When movement is synchronized with others (think Zumba or line dancing), endorphins increase. These feel-good peptides are part of social bonding.[2] Dance, no matter the sort, can help you get out of your head and into your body. So move to the groove and feel your mood improve.

How to Use This Remedy

If you're taking a dance class, that's great. If not, consider joining the fun, but that's not required to derive benefits. Think like my event participant who made the "one step forward, two steps back" scenario a routine. A few dance steps as you wait for your coffee to brew each morning can be a short, spontaneous session with benefits. Try free-form with steps forward and back or gently sway, even in a chair. Do the twist, pump your arms, or do the hokey pokey and turn yourself around. If you begin by practicing even the simplest forms of dance when you're not necessarily lost in a ruminative loop, you'll be more prepared when you are.

Starting today, whenever you find your mind shifting into negative overdrive, *dance*. Use group dance to get the benefits of synchronized movement. YouTube videos featuring a group can help. Or imagine dancing with a friend.

This tool is all yours, whenever, wherever, however. There is only one rule: On a regular basis, *bust a move*. In a chair, around your kitchen, or under a disco ball—you can dance through life.

Practice this technique over the next several days and write about the experience. Did you feel happier after dancing? What type of dance did you choose? How did you move? Were you reminded of past dance experiences either with a partner, in a group, or on your own? How can you make more room for dancing in your life?

> "Pirouetting and setting they cross and advance
> In a ripple of laughter, and pair for a dance."
> —*R. C. Lehmann* (1856-1929)

Remedy 39

Viva Las *Vagus!*

Initial Notes

From my childhood, I remember one aunt's home as a restful place. Immediately upon entering, a sense of serenity wrapped around me like a soothing blanket. Clean, calm, and with zero chaos. My memories include my aunt humming as she dusted her things, served meals, or outlined activities for the cousins. Recently, I learned how humming calms—and immediately longed to revisit those moments in her home.

Whether singing words, simply humming, or even whistling a tune, this remedy replaces rumination with rhythm.

Why This Remedy Works

Singing, humming, and whistling disrupt negative thoughts. They also vibrate the vocal cords and increase the length of exhalations, thus stimulating your vagus nerve. As the Introduction and several of the Remedies mention, vagus nerve stimulation enhances nervous system resilience and helps you relax.

How to Use This Remedy

There's a reason why people whistle while they work. It lifts their mood and adds levity to what may otherwise be boring or difficult tasks. Same goes for thinking. Whenever your mind starts to churn, whistle, hum, or sing.

If a tune comes to mind, choose it. If not, make one up. Take your lowest thoughts and turn them into a song—a funeral dirge, a spiritual hymn, or a jaunty dance beat. The words don't even have to make sense. When you relax and let yourself go, you may be surprised by what emerges. A tune may transport you, mentally, to another time and place. Rhyming words or belted-out thoughts can connect with deeper memories or meanings.

Insert new words to the tune of a lullaby, a commercial jingle, or something you loved as a kid. Voice the tones of well-known theme songs. Amidst drama or chaos? Hum *Twilight Zone* beats. Ruminating over a tense upcoming visit? Mimic the shark attack beats from the classic movie *Jaws*. This remedy is meant to be easy and fun.

Over the next several days, make it a practice to whistle, sing, or hum as you work, play, or think. Use in times of need or practice this remedy to make a routine of stimulating your vagus nerve. Your nervous system (and perhaps your funny bone) will benefit. As always, write about the experience. What helped? How were you distracted? Did unexpected or meaningful words come out? Our singing voice, our humming, or the tune we whistle can free what's stuck.

_____

_____

_____

_____

_____

_____

_____

_____

_____

Remedy 40

Learning Curve, The Wrap-Up

Initial Notes

Congratulations! You're almost through the workbook and are prepared to transfer what you've learned from interacting with the exercises to your life going forward.

How Learning Transfer Works

The concept of "learning transfer" is a well-known benefit of whatever we gain. Whether what we learn is via formal education, something we read, study, or experiment with, we naturally transfer the gained skills or knowledge to what we encounter into the real world. We learn to balance, to stand, to walk, and then to run. It's the same with our inner world. When a grounding technique works well for one rumination trigger, we transfer that knowledge to other situations that cause us to fret. We keep learning what works.

Throughout the book, you've seen exercises applied to example circumstances and have been encouraged to transfer their use to your own. You've been guided into "learning transfer" all along. Now, you can take the knowledge you've gained through these pages, along with your experimentation and journaling, and apply the techniques even further.

Worrying about an upcoming meeting with difficult people? Lean on your new knowledge about mental time travel and disrupt your thinking. Need a quick pick-me-up to clear your head? Combine forward physical movement with metaphorical affirmations. Feeling stuck in a woe-is-me mire? Gain some distance with questions or statements to "you."

As life unfolds and our feelings and routines change, new ruminative loops may try to make inroads. You're prepared and will transfer all you learned to help yourself. Plus, you'll gain new knowledge as you go—and transfer that learning to new situations as well.

What you learn in one domain works for another. Many of the techniques you've tried will apply to real-world moments. It's not just before or after mind bogs that benefit. A cyclic sigh helps with almost any tense moment. Fresh eyes assist you in managing your workload just as well as a new perspective helps you seize upon a novel opening for that book you want to write. You've done the learning, and if you review your notes and practice, the knowledge will bubble forth as you apply it in new ways.

Perhaps you have already noticed times when you've drawn upon what you've learned as you've interacted with the workbook. Take a moment now to write about this. Also consider any upcoming circumstances where you might transfer your learning to better cope or perform.

Measure Your Progress

Which of the skills covered in Remedies 32–39 have you experimented with? To the left of the listed remedies, check off each you've tried.

Review your notes and reflect upon each experience. If needed, run through the steps again. Then, using a scale of 0–10, write the number that best represents your experience with each technique (on the line to the right).

_____ **32: Tune in and Tune Out** *(Using all of your senses.)* _____

_____ **33: P-R-O-C-E-E-D** *(A process to create a positive shift.)* _____

_____ **34: Bend Your Ear** *(Auricular massage to stimulate your vagus nerve.)* _____

_____ **35: Worse-Case Scenario** *(Reality-based problem solving.)* _____

_____ **36: Your B-F-F** *(Big picture thinking.)* _____

_____ **37: Real Eyes for Peace** *(Adjust how and what you look at for peace.)* _____

_____ **38: Bust a Move** *(The power of dance.)* _____

_____ **39: Viva Las Vagus!** *(Sing, hum, or whistle to stimulate the vagus nerve.)* _____

Catch Up or Toss

Now is the time to try any techniques you skipped or didn't fully attend to. Also consider any *Additional Tips and Techniques* boxes you neglected.

What Didn't Help?

Use the lines here to reflect on any exercises you didn't find helpful.

_____

_____

_____

Favorites So Far

Using your ratings of Remedies 32–39, note the tools you found most helpful. Consider why these worked. What did you like about them? How easy were they to implement and remember?

Reflecting here will provide insight into the best times for you to experiment, as well as how to make the techniques more your own. After journaling about your favorites, use the last block of lines in this *Learning Curve* to record the titles of your favorites among Remedies 32–39.

_____

_____

_____

_____

_____

_____

_____

_____

_____

_____

_____

My Go-Tos

My Notes

Remedy 41

Congratulate Yourself!

You've come a long way and it's time to celebrate your progress. Write a few short congratulatory thoughts to yourself here. In what way did sticking with the exercises make you proud? How did you follow through when an exercise was challenging? How have you grown? What's a main takeaway from your experience with *Rumination Remedies*? How can you celebrate your progress?

_____
_____
_____
_____
_____
_____
_____

A Final Thought

Changing habits and taking on better ones requires effort and patience. If you find yourself backsliding, notice with kindness. Give yourself grace. Well-worn grooves in thinking can be like creases in a cotton napkin that's been lying folded, perhaps for decades, in a drawer. More than one pass of a hot steam iron is required to straighten them out. Likewise, changing your unhelpful thoughts will require practice, humility, and grit. One thing's for certain: Your peace is worth the effort.

Completing Your Go-To List

To help you move forward and support your peace of mind, you'll find the remedies listed in the table below. Refer to the go-to lists you created at the end of each *Learning Curve*, find those titles in the table, and put a check to the left of each one you chose. To the right of each remedy, you'll see a place to mark the score you gave each one. Copy the scores into the spaces provided. Then sort your go-to remedies by highest to lowest scores into the space titled "My Go-Tos" at the end. Add page numbers for convenient review. These are your all-time favorites and those you'll want to turn to most often to practice and commit to memory.

_____ **4: Watch Your Tone** *(Identify and improve how you talk to yourself.)* _____

_____ **5: Who's That You're Talking To?** *(Name yourself in your thoughts.)* _____

_____ **6: Wee-Hour Check-In** *(Notice your physical feelings.)* _____

_____ **7: Shift into Neutral** *(Refocus on basic plans for the immediate future.)* _____

_____ **8: The Shake Break** *(Expel excess energy by shaking it off.)* _____

_____ **9: Pattern Interrupt** *(Disrupt negative thinking with something new.)* _____

_____ **10: Cherished Evidence** *(Immerse in the present and later savor.)* _____

_____ **11: Chill Out** *(Calm your nervous system by applying cold.)* _____

_____ **13: Making Tomorrow Real** *(Get in touch with your future self.)* _____

_____ **14: N-E-W** *(Create an acronym and use it to help.)* _____

_____ **15: You're Here Now, and Safe** *(Grounding Methods.)* _____

_____ **16: Awestruck** *(The power of nature.)* _____

REMEDY 41: Congratulate Yourself! 215

_____ **17: Fresh Eyes** *(Seeing things from a new perspective)* _____

_____ **18: What Would Batman, Jesus, or the Dalai Lama Do?** *(Using alter egos.)* _____

_____ **19: Thrival, It's in Your Genes** *(Leaning on the resilience of ancestors.)* _____

_____ **20: A Routine to Remember** *(Behavioral rituals for comfort and confidence.)* _____

_____ **21: The Mother's Touch** *("Earthing" techniques for well-being.)* _____

_____ **23: Pour it Out** *(Journaling for helpful insight.)* _____

_____ **24: Say it to the Dolls** *(Releasing your worries.)* _____

_____ **25: Normalize** *(You're not so different or alone.)* _____

_____ **26: *Solvitur Ambulando*** *(Physical and metaphorical momentum.)* _____

_____ **27: Touchstones and Talismans** *(Symbols of positive perception.)* _____

_____ **28: Tidy Up** *(External order for internal order.)* _____

_____ **29: In Flow** *(Losing track of yourself and time.)* _____

_____ **30: A Sigh of Relief** *(Using a natural form of stress-reducing breathwork.)* _____

_____ **32: Tune in and Tune Out** *(Using all of your senses.)* _____

_____ **33: P-R-O-C-E-E-D** *(A process to create a positive shift.)* _____

_____ **34: Bend Your Ear** *(Auricular massage to stimulate your vagus nerve.)* _____

_____ **35: Worse-Case Scenario** *(Reality-based problem solving.)* _____

_____ **36: Your B-F-F** *(Big picture thinking.)* _____

_____ **37: Real Eyes for Peace** *(Adjust how and what you look at for peace.)* _____

_____ **38: Bust a Move** *(The power of dance.)* _____

_____ **39: *Viva Las Vagus!*** *(Sing, hum, or whistle to stimulate the vagus nerve.)* _____

My Go-Tos

About the Author

Sheri McGregor holds a Master's Degree in Human Behavior and has been writing and life coaching for more than two decades. She loves her work to help people reclaim their self-worth and step courageously toward peace—and their dreams. Some of her advanced training and certifications include brain-based coaching, end-of-life and sacred passage work, aging-related wellness and integrative health from a depth psychology perspective, and the neuroscience of change. Sheri is most well-known for her work with parents of estranged adult children. Find out more about her at **www.SheriMcGregor.com**

ENDNOTES

Remedy 2: Your Turnaround

1. DeSteno, D. (2018). *Emotional success: The power of gratitude, compassion, and pride.* Houghton Mifflin Harcourt.

2. Park, S. H., Lim, B. S., & Lim, S. T. (2020). The effects of self-talk on shooting athletes' motivation. *Journal of Sports Science & Medicine, 19*(3), 517–521. https://pubmed.ncbi.nlm.nih.gov/32874104

3. Sadri Damirchi, E., Mojarrad, A., Pireinaladin, S., & Grjibovski, A. M. (2020). The role of self-talk in predicting death anxiety, obsessive-compulsive disorder, and coping strategies in the face of coronavirus disease (COVID-19). *Iranian Journal of Psychiatry, 15*(3), 182–188. https://doi.org/10.18502/ijps.v15i3.3810

Remedy 3: Learning Curve: Your Wi-Fi

1. Matthews, G. (2007). The impact of writing goals on goal attainment: An eight-month study. *International Journal of Behavioral Science, 2*(1), 69–79.

2. Locke, E. A., & Latham, G. P. (2006). New directions in goal-setting theory. *Current Directions in Psychological Science, 15*(5), 265–268. https://doi.org/10.1111/j.1467-8721.2006.00449.x

Remedy 5: Who's That You're Talking To?

1. Moser, J. S., Dougherty, A., Mattson, W. I., Haller, S. P., Fischer, N., & Kross, E. (2017). Third-person self-talk facilitates emotion regulation without engaging cognitive control: Converging evidence from ERP and fMRI. *Scientific Reports, 7,* 4519. https://doi.org/10.1038/s41598-017-04047-3

2. Kross, E., Bruehlman-Senecal, E., Park, J., Burson, A., Dougherty, A., Shablack, H., Bremner, R., Moser, J., & Ayduk, O. (2014). Self-talk as a regulatory mechanism: How you do it matters. *Journal of Personality and Social Psychology, 106*(2), 304–324. https://doi.org/10.1037/a0035173

Remedy 6: Wee-Hour Check-In

1. Fogel, A. (2021). *Restorative embodiment and resilience: A guide to disrupt habits, create inner peace, deepen relationships, and feel greater presence.* North Atlantic Books.

Remedy 7: Shift into Neutral

1. Suddendorf, T., & Corballis, M. C. (1997). Mental time travel and the evolution of the human mind. *Genetic, social, and general psychology monographs, 123*(2), 133–167.

2. Sansone, R. A., & Sansone, L. A. (2012). Rumination: Relationships with physical health. *Innovations in Clinical Neuroscience, 9*(2), 29–34. https://pubmed.ncbi.nlm.nih.gov/22468242

3. Quoidbach, J., Wood, A. M., & Hansenne, M. (2009). Back to the future: The effect of daily practice of mental time travel into the future on happiness and anxiety. *The Journal of Positive Psychology, 4*(5), 349–355. https://doi.org/10.1080/17439760902992365

Remedy 8: The Shake Break
1. Koch, S. C., Riege, R. F. F., Tisborn, K., Biondo, J., Martin, L., & Beelmann, A. (2019). Effects of dance movement therapy and dance on health-related psychological outcomes: A meta-analysis update. *Frontiers in Psychology, 10*, 1806. https://doi.org/10.3389/fpsyg.2019.01806

Remedy 9: Pattern Interrupt
1. Wang, L., & Miller, L. (2023). Assessment and disruption of ruminative episodes to enhance mobile cognitive behavioral therapy just-in-time adaptive interventions in clinical depression: Pilot randomized controlled trial. *JMIR Formative Research, 7*, e37270. https://doi.org/10.2196/37270

Remedy 10: Cherished Evidence
1. Smith, J. L., & Hollinger-Smith, L. (2015). Savoring, resilience, and psychological well-being in older adults. *Aging & Mental Health, 19*(3), 192–200. https://doi.org/10.1080/13607863.2014.986647

Remedy 11: Message to Self—Chill Out
1. Jungmann, M., Vencatachellum, S., Van Ryckeghem, D., & Vögele, C. (2018). Effects of cold stimulation on cardiac-vagal activation in healthy participants: Randomized controlled trial. *JMIR Formative Research, 2*(2), e10257. https://doi.org/10.2196/10257

Remedy 12: Learning Curve, a Five-Star Review
1. Sherrington, T. (2019). *Rosenshine's principles in action*. John Catt Educational.

Remedy 13: Making Tomorrow Real
1. Ersner-Hershfield, H., Wimmer, G. E., & Knutson, B. (2009). Saving for the future self: Neural measures of future self-continuity predict temporal discounting. *Social Cognitive and Affective Neuroscience, 4*(1), 85–92. https://doi.org/10.1093/scan/nsn042

2. Ahmed, S. P., Somerville, L. H., & Sebastian, C. L. (2018). Using temporal distancing to regulate emotion in adolescence: Modulation by reactive aggression. *Cognition and Emotion, 32*(4), 812–826. https://doi.org/10.1080/02699931.2017.1358698

3. Bruehlman-Senecal, E., & Ayduk, O. (2015). This too shall pass: Temporal distance and the regulation of emotional distress. *Journal of Personality and Social Psychology, 108*(2), 356–375. https://doi.org/10.1037/a0038324

4. Macrae, C. N., Mitchell, J. P., Tait, K. A., McNamara, D. L., Golubickis, M., Topalidis, P. P., & Christian, B. M. (2015). Turning I into me: Imagining your future self. *Consciousness and Cognition, 37*, 207–213. https://doi.org/10.1016/j.concog.2015.09.009

5. Ersner-Hershfield, H., Garton, T. G., Ballard, K., Samanez-Larkin, G. R., & Knutson, B. (2009). Don't stop thinking about tomorrow: Individual differences in future self-continuity account for saving. *Judgment and Decision Making, 4*(4), 280–286.

6. Whitbourne, S. K., & Sneed, J. R. (2002). The paradox of well-being, identity processes, and stereotype threat: Ageism and its potential relationships to the self in later life. In T. D. Nelson (Ed.), *Ageism: Stereotyping and prejudice against older persons* (2nd ed., pp. 247–273). MIT Press.

Remedy 16: Awestruck

1. Nisbet, E. K., Zelenski, J. M., & Murphy, S. A. (2011). Happiness is in our nature: Exploring nature relatedness as a contributor to subjective well-being. *Journal of Happiness Studies, 12*, 303–322.

2. Lopes, S., Lima, M., & Silva, K. (2020). Nature can get it out of your mind: The rumination-reducing effects of contact with nature and the mediating role of awe and mood. *Journal of Environmental Psychology, 71*, 101489. https://doi.org/10.1016/j.jenvp.2020.101489

3. Muir, J. (1938). *John of the mountains: The unpublished journals of John Muir* (E. W. Teale, Ed.). Houghton Mifflin. (Original work published on p. 295, quoted in *The wilderness world of John Muir*, p. 313)

Remedy 17: Fresh Eyes

1. Rigo, P., Kim, P., Esposito, G., Putnick, D. L., Venuti, P., & Bornstein, M. H. (2019). Specific maternal brain responses to their own child's face: An fMRI meta-analysis. *Developmental review : DR, 51*, 58–69. https://doi.org/10.1016/j.dr.2018.12.001

2. Blackwell, S. E. (2019). Mental imagery: From basic research to clinical practice. *Journal of Psychotherapy Integration, 29*(3), 235. https://doi.org/10.1037/int0000181

3. Murphy, S. E., O'Donoghue, M. C., Drazich, E. H., Blackwell, S. E., Nobre, A. C., & Holmes, E. A. (2015). Imagining a brighter future: The effect of positive imagery training on mood, prospective mental imagery, and emotional bias in older adults. *Psychiatry Research, 230*(1), 36–43. https://doi.org/10.1016/j.psychres.2015.07.069

Remedy 18: What Would Batman, Jesus, or the Dalai Lama Do?

1. White, R. E., Prager, E. O., Schaefer, C., Kross, E., Duckworth, A. L., & Carlson, S. M. (2017). The "Batman effect": Improving perseverance in young children. *Child Development, 88*(5), 1563–1571. https://doi.org/10.1111/cdev.12695

Remedy 19: Thrival: It's in Your Genes

1. Chadborn, D., & Reysen, S. (2018). Moved by the masses: A social identity perspective on inspiration. *Current Psychology, 37*(3), 625–631. https://doi.org/10.1007/s12144-016-9545-9

2. Moser, J. S., Dougherty, A., Mattson, W. I., Haller, S. P., Fischer, N., & Kross, E. (2017). Third-person self-talk facilitates emotion regulation without engaging cognitive control: Converging evidence from ERP and fMRI. *Scientific Reports, 7*, 4519. https://doi.org/10.1038/s41598-017-04047-3

3. Kross, E., Bruehlman-Senecal, E., Park, J., Burson, A., Dougherty, A., Shablack, H., Bremner, R., Moser, J., & Ayduk, O. (2014). Self-talk as a regulatory mechanism: How you do it matters. *Journal of Personality and Social Psychology, 106*(2), 304–324. https://doi.org/10.1037/a0035173

4. Dolcos, S., & Albarracin, D. (2014). The inner speech of behavioral regulation: Intentions and task performance strengthen when you talk to yourself as a You. *European Journal of Social Psychology, 44*(6), 636–642. https://doi.org/10.1002/ejsp.2048

Remedy 20: A Routine to Remember

1. Brooks, A. W., Schroeder, J., Risen, J. L., Gino, F., Galinsky, A. D., Norton, M. I., & Schweitzer, M. E. (2016). Don't stop believing: Rituals improve performance by decreasing anxiety. *Organizational Behavior and Human Decision Processes, 137*, 71–85.

2. Lang, M., Krátký, J., Shaver, J. H., Jerotijević, D., & Xygalatas, D. (2015). Effects of anxiety on spontaneous ritualized behavior. *Current Biology, 25*, 1892–1897.

3. Shore, B. (2023). *The hidden power of rituals: The journey of a lifetime*. The MIT Press.

4. Boyer, P., & Liénard, P. (2006). Precaution systems and ritualized behavior. *Behavioral and Brain Sciences, 29*(6), 635–641.

5. Hirsch, J. B., Mar, R. A., & Peterson, J. B. (2012). Psychological entropy: A framework for understanding uncertainty-related anxiety. *Psychological Review, 119*, 304–320.

6. Boyer, P., & Liénard, P. (2008). Ritual behavior in obsessive and normal individuals: Moderating anxiety and reorganizing the flow of action. *Current Directions in Psychological Science, 17*, 291–294.

7. Van Dillen, L. F., & Koole, S. L. (2007). Clearing the mind: A working memory model of distraction from negative mood. *Emotion, 7*, 715–723.

8. Anastasi, M. W., & Newberg, A. B. (2008). A preliminary study of the acute effects of religious ritual on anxiety. *The Journal of Alternative and Complementary Medicine, 14*(2), 163–165.

9. Critcher, C. R., & Dunning, D. (2014). Self-affirmations provide a broader perspective on self-threat. *Personality and Social Psychology Bulletin, 41*, 3–18.

10. Crum, A. J., & Langer, E. J. (2007). Mind-set matters: Exercise and the placebo effect. *Psychological Science, 18*(2), 165–171.

Remedy 21: The Mother's Touch

1. Be Healthy Now. (n.d.). *Grounding and mental health: Benefits and practices to feel better*. https://www.behealthynow.co.uk/healthy-mind/grounding-and-mental-health/

2. Chevalier, G., Sinatra, S. T., Oschman, J. L., Sokal, K., & Sokal, P. (2012). Earthing: Health implications of reconnecting the human body to the Earth's surface electrons. *Journal of Environmental and Public Health, 2012*, Article 291541, 1–8. https://doi.org/10.1155/2012/291541

3. Sinatra, S. T., Sinatra, D. S., Sinatra, S. W., & Chevalier, G. (2023). Grounding – The universal anti-inflammatory remedy. *Biomedical Journal, 46*(1), 11–16. https://doi.org/10.1016/j.bj.2022.12.002

4. Ghaly, M., & Teplitz, D. (2004). The biologic effects of grounding the human body during sleep as measured by cortisol levels and subjective reporting of sleep, pain, and stress. *Journal of Alternative and Complementary Medicine, 10*(5), 767–776. https://doi.org/10.1089/acm.2004.10.767

5. Wilder, T. (2025). *The grounding healing Bible: Unlock the power of earthing to relieve chronic pain, reduce stress, achieve deep sleep, boost energy, enhance mental performance, and transform your well-being naturally*. Independently published.

Remedy 22: Learning Curve, Building Bridges

1. Wells, A. (2000). *Emotional disorders and metacognition: Innovative cognitive therapy.* Wiley.

2. Dweck, C. S. (2006). *Mindset: The new psychology of success.* Random House.

3. Zimmerman, B. J. (2002). Becoming a self-regulated learner: An overview. *Theory Into Practice, 41*(2), 64–70. https://doi.org/10.1207/s15430421tip4102_2

4. Bransford, J. D., Brown, A. L., & Cocking, R. R. (Eds.). (2000). *How people learn: Brain, mind, experience, and school* (Expanded ed.). National Academy Press. https://doi.org/10.17226/9853

5. National Academies of Sciences, Engineering, and Medicine. (2018). *How people learn II: Learners, contexts, and cultures.* The National Academies Press. https://doi.org/10.17226/24783

6. Papageorgiou, C., & Wells, A. (2003). An empirical test of a clinical metacognitive model of rumination and depression. *Cognitive Therapy and Research, 27*(3), 261–273. https://doi.org/10.1023/A:1023962332399

Remedy 23: Pour It Out

1. Baikie, K. A., & Wilhelm, K. (2005). Emotional and physical health benefits of expressive writing. *Advances in Psychiatric Treatment, 11*(5), 338–346. https://doi.org/10.1192/apt.11.5.338

Remedy 26: *Solvitur Ambulando*

1. Webb, C. E., Rossignac-Milon, M., & Higgins, E. T. (2017). Stepping forward together: Could walking facilitate interpersonal conflict resolution? *American Psychologist, 72*(4), 374–385. https://doi.org/10.1037/a0040431

2. Oppezzo, M., & Schwartz, D. L. (2014). Give your ideas some legs: The positive effect of walking on creative thinking. *Journal of Experimental Psychology: Learning, Memory, and Cognition, 40*(4), 1142–1152. https://doi.org/10.1037/a0036577

3. Puterman, E., O'Donovan, A., Adler, N. E., Tomiyama, A. J., Kemeny, M., Wolkowitz, O. M., & Epel, E. (2011). Physical activity moderates effects of stressor-induced rumination on cortisol reactivity. *Psychosomatic Medicine, 73*(7), 604–611. https://doi.org/10.1097/PSY.0b013e318229e1e0

4. Lakoff, G., & Johnson, M. (1980). *Metaphors we live by.* University of Chicago Press.

5. Landau, M. J., Meier, B. P., & Keefer, L. A. (2010). A metaphor-enriched social cognition. *Psychological Bulletin, 136*(6), 1045–1067. https://doi.org/10.1037/a0020970

Remedy 28: Tidy Up

1. Bodrij, F. F., Andeweg, S. M., Prevoo, M. J. L., Rippe, R. C. A., & Alink, L. R. A. (2021). The causal effect of household chaos on stress and caregiving: An experimental study. *Comprehensive Psychoneuroendocrinology, 8*, 100090. https://doi.org/10.1016/j.cpnec.2021.100090

2. De Veer, A. J. E., De Groot, K., & Verkaik, R. (2022). Home care for patients with dirty homes: A qualitative study of the problems experienced by nurses and possible solutions. *BMC Health Services Research, 22*(1), 592. https://doi.org/10.1186/s12913-022-07988-2

3. Ognjanovic, S., Thüring, M., Murphy, R. O., & Hölscher, C. (2019). Display clutter and its effects on visual attention distribution and financial risk judgment. *Applied Ergonomics, 80*, 168–174. https://doi.org/10.1016/j.apergo.2019.05.008

4. Sorrell, J. M. (2020). Tidying up: Good for the aging brain. *Journal of Psychosocial Nursing and Mental Health Services, 58*(4), 16–18. https://doi.org/10.3928/02793695-20200316-02

5. Frost, R. O., & Gross, R. C. (1993). The hoarding of possessions. *Behaviour Research and Therapy, 31*(4), 367–381.

6. Tolin, D. F., Frost, R. O., Steketee, G., Gray, K. D., & Fitch, K. E. (2008). The economic and social burden of compulsive hoarding. *Psychiatry Research, 160*(2), 200–211. https://doi.org/10.1016/j.psychres.2007.08.008

7. McGregor, S. (2021). *Beyond done with the crying: More answers and advice for parents of estranged adult children.* Sowing Creek Press.

Remedy 29: In Flow

1. Mosing, M. A., Butkovic, A., & Ullén, F. (2018). Can flow experiences be protective of work-related depressive symptoms and burnout? A genetically informative approach. *Journal of Affective Disorders, 226*, 6–11. https://doi.org/10.1016/j.jad.2017.09.017

2. Gaston, E., Ullén, F., Wesseldijk, L. W., & Mosing, M. A. (2024). Can flow proneness be protective against mental and cardiovascular health problems? A genetically informed prospective cohort study. *Translational Psychiatry, 14*(1), Article 144. https://doi.org/10.1038/s41398-024-02855-6

3. Yaden, D. B., Haidt, J., Hood, R. W., Vago, D. R., & Newberg, A. B. (2017). The varieties of self-transcendent experience. *Review of General Psychology, 21*(2), 143–160. https://doi.org/10.1037/gpr0000102

4. Csikszentmihalyi, M. (1975). *Beyond boredom and anxiety.* Jossey-Bass.

5. Ullén, F., de Manzano, Ö., Theorell, T., & Harmat, L. (2010). The physiology of effortless attention: Correlates of state flow and flow proneness. In B. Bruya (Ed.), *Effortless attention: A new perspective in the cognitive science of attention and action* (pp. 205–217). MIT Press.

Remedy 30: A Sigh of Relief

1. Ramirez, J. M. (2014). The integrative role of the sigh in psychology, physiology, pathology, and neurobiology. *Progress in Brain Research, 209*, 91–129. https://doi.org/10.1016/B978-0-444-63274-6.00006-0

2. Sody, A. N., Kiderman, A., Biton, A., & Furst, A. (2008). Sigh syndrome: Is it a sign of trouble? *The Journal of Family Practice, 57*, E1–E5.

3. Vlemincx, E., Van Diest, I., De Peuter, S., Bresseleers, J., Bogaerts, K., Fannes, S., Li, W., & Van den Bergh, O. (2009). Why do you sigh? Sigh rate during induced stress and relief. *Psychophysiology, 46*(5), 1005–1013. https://doi.org/10.1111/j.1469-8986.2009.00842.x

4. Vlemincx, E., Taelman, J., Van Diest, I., & Van den Bergh, O. (2010a). Take a deep breath: The relief effect of spontaneous and instructed sighs. *Physiology & Behavior, 101*(1), 67–73. https://doi.org/10.1016/j.physbeh.2010.04.015

5. Vlemincx, E., Van Diest, I., Lehrer, P. M., Aubert, A. E., & Van den Bergh, O. (2010b). Respiratory variability preceding and following sighs: A resetter hypothesis. *Biological Psychology, 84*(1), 82–87. https://doi.org/10.1016/j.biopsycho.2009.09.002

6. Vlemincx, E., Taelman, J., De Peuter, S., Van Diest, I., & Van den Bergh, O. (2011). Sigh rate and respiratory variability during mental load and sustained attention. *Psychophysiology, 48*(1), 117–120. https://doi.org/10.1111/j.1469-8986.2010.01043.x

7. Vlemincx, E., Abelson, J. L., Lehrer, P. M., Davenport, P. W., Van Diest, I., & Van den Bergh, O. (2013a). Respiratory variability and sighing: A psychophysiological reset model. *Biological Psychology, 93*(1), 24–32. https://doi.org/10.1016/j.biopsycho.2012.12.001

8. Vlemincx, E., Vigo, D., Vansteenwegen, D., Van den Bergh, O., & Van Diest, I. (2013b). Do not worry, be mindful: Effects of induced worry and mindfulness on respiratory variability in a nonanxious population. *International Journal of Psychophysiology, 87*(2), 147–151. https://doi.org/10.1016/j.ijpsycho.2012.12.002

9. Balban, M. Y., et al. (2023). Brief structured respiration practices enhance mood and reduce physiological arousal. *Cell Reports Medicine, 4*(1), Article 00895. https://doi.org/10.1016/j.xcrm.2022.100895

Remedy 31: Learning Curve, Body in Mind
1. Glenberg, A. M., Witt, J. K., & Metcalfe, J. (2013). From the revolution to embodiment: 25 years of cognitive psychology. *Perspectives on Psychological Science, 8*(5), 573–585.

Remedy 32: Tune in and Tune Out
1. McGregor, S. (2021). *Beyond done with the crying: More answers and advice for parents of estranged adult children.* Sowing Creek Press.

2. McGregor, S. (n.d.). *Kneaded.* RejectedParents.net. https://www.rejectedparents.net/kneaded/

Remedy 34: Bend Your Ear?
1. Choi, S., & Kim, B. (2024). Effect of auriculotherapy on stress: A systematic review and meta-analysis. *Journal of Holistic Nursing.* Advance online publication. https://doi.org/10.1177/08980101241257138

2. Wu, Y., Zou, C., Liu, X., Wu, X., & Lin, Q. (2014). Auricular acupressure helps improve sleep quality for severe insomnia in maintenance hemodialysis patients: A pilot study. *The Journal of Alternative and Complementary Medicine, 20*(5), 356–363. https://doi.org/10.1089/acm.2013.0319

3. University of Oklahoma College of Medicine. (n.d.). *Ear-clip stimulation of vagus nerve shows promise as POTS treatment, according to OU College of Medicine study.* https://medicine.ouhsc.edu/news/article/ear-clip-stimulation-of-vagus-nerve-shows-promise-as-pots-treatment-according-to-ou-college-of-medicine-study

4. TENSPros. (n.d.). *The ultimate guide to vagus nerve stimulation.* https://www.tenspros.com/the-ultimate-guide-to-vagus-nerve-stimulation

Remedy 36: Your B-F-F

1. MacBride, L. (2015, November 25). *Eye of the heron*. Eye on Environment. https://eyeonenvironment.com/2015/11/25/eye-of-the-heron/

Remedy 37: Real Eyes for Peace

1. *Secrets to surviving stressful times*. (2021, January). *Scientific American Mind, 32*(1), 14. https://doi.org/10.1038/scientificamericanmind0121-14

2. Be Inspired. (2020, December 10). *"Your behaviour won't be the same" | Dr. Andrew Huberman (Stanford neuroscientist)* [Video]. YouTube. https://www.youtube.com/watch?v=xZVw-9ThmSM

3. Mark Bell's Power Project. (2021, September 15). *Andrew Huberman explains the benefits of lateral eye movements* [Video]. YouTube. https://www.youtube.com/watch?v=fHHQ0dJ0rcQ

Remedy 38: Bust a Move

1. Koch, S. C., Riege, R. F. F., Tisborn, K., Biondo, J., Martin, L., & Beelmann, A. (2019). Effects of dance movement therapy and dance on health-related psychological outcomes: A meta-analysis update. *Frontiers in Psychology, 10*, Article 1806. https://doi.org/10.3389/fpsyg.2019.01806

2. Fong Yan, A., Nicholson, L. L., Ward, R. E., Hiller, C. E., Dovey, K., Parker, H. M., Low, L. F., Moyle, G., & Chan, C. (2024). The effectiveness of dance interventions on psychological and cognitive health outcomes compared with other forms of physical activity: A systematic review with meta-analysis. *Sports Medicine, 54*(5), 1179–1205. https://doi.org/10.1007/s40279-023-01990-2

"Be like the bird that, pausing in her flight awhile on boughs too slight, feels them give way beneath her, yet sings, knowing she hath wings."
—*Victor Hugo* (1802–1885)

www.ingramcontent.com/pod-product-compliance
Lightning Source LLC
Chambersburg PA
CBHW051403070526
44584CB00023B/3277